Buster Keaton

David Robinson

Indiana University Press
Bloomington and London

The Cinema One series is published by
Indiana University Press
in association with *Sight and Sound*
and the Education Department of the
British Film Institute

Copyright © 1969 by David Robinson

First United States publication 1969
Second printing 1970

Library of Congress catalog card number: 68–66394
SBN: 253–10950–7 [CL.]
     253–10951–5 [PA.]

Printed in Great Britain

Contents

1: Buster

Buster Keaton—or Joseph Francis Keaton as he is identified on his birth certificate and his gravestone— must be reckoned among the great figures in the arts of the twentieth century. He never for a moment thought of himself in such terms; and was deeply embarrassed and mistrustful when other people did so. Like everyone else in the film business in the years 1917 to 1929, during which he made something like twenty-four hours of silent film—a dozen features and thirty or so shorts—he thought of himself simply as a hard-working and commercially lucky knockabout entertainer, an old vaudeville pro who had found a fortunate niche in the film business. Forty or fifty years on, and away from the million-dollar market-place in which his talent was bought, sold and ultimately trampled, we see him differently.

Of course he still reaches us because he is incomparably, irresistibly, unalterably funny: there is nothing esoteric or mysterious about the continuing appeal of Keaton. His invention was torrential: he never really repeated himself or imitated himself through all these three dozen films. If he did play a gag more than once it was generally in order to do it better or to build upon it, never because he needed to be parsimonious with his resources. This much was always clear; but today we are in a better position to appreciate his instinctive mastery of the film medium. He used film as freely and as easily as ordinary speech, and as unselfconsciously. It is because the cinema was to him an

7

Keaton in vaudeville, *c.* 1900

entirely personal means of expression, untouched by modes and period styles, that his films have not dated at all. Even their silence has more the appearance of artistic choice than of technical restriction.

Throughout practically all his work there is an astonishing harmony and *correctness*. Of course he made mistakes and suffered failures like any artist; but the passages in Keaton's work which we (and probably he) might have wished different are astonishingly few—particularly in the context of a technique as chancy as film-making. 'Good taste' suggests a quality that is drab and inhibited; but as Keaton possessed it, in the sense of a rightness of choice and selection, it was an instinct of genius.

Keaton's greatest creation, of course, was himself. He appeared in many different roles: father and son, millionaire and bum, half-wit and scholar, cowhand and stockbroker, fugitive and man-about-town, ardent lover and oppressed husband. He was a fine and conscientious actor, and gave all these characters their own validity. Yet ultimately they all fuse into one figure, a small, solitary, solemn animal with a face of other-worldly beauty and great melancholy unsmiling eyes that gaze unflinchingly outwards upon a world which must always dwarf him, but cannot diminish him; because behind those eyes there is a soul.

If it were ever possible to explain genius, something might be learnt from the unique circumstances of his life. He had the good fortune—rare in a civilised twentieth-century society like America —entirely to escape formal education. He was born straight into his work, and never really knew any other life. From the age of two or three, the whole purpose of being was, for him, to make people laugh. For many years there was nothing to distract him from this intense concentration. He did not even have to worry—as the young Chaplin did, for instance—about the ordinary problems of daily existence: the family vaudeville act was in good work and fairly prosperous almost from the time of his birth. So the creation of comedy was inborn, instinctive and exclusive. It was his whole life, which is why the withdrawal of the means of creation in the middle years of his life was a circumstance of especial tragedy.

The circumstances of his life were particularly favourable to the development of his gifts; but they can still not explain the gifts themselves, the extent of his creativity and the depth and durability of his creation. Nothing, ultimately, can explain, which is why it is with hesitation that yet another monograph on Buster Keaton is offered. The object of this book is to deal exclusively with the films themselves: to describe them, to analyse their effect in so far as it can be analysed rather than simply experienced and enjoyed; to collect together as much as can be discovered or seems relevant about the circumstances in which they were made and about Keaton's approach to them and his working method. Biographical material has been avoided except where it seems directly relevant: Keaton's life history has in any case been exhaustively and definitively covered by Rudi Blesh's admirable biography and, less methodically, by the comedian's own autobiography. Indeed the only point in supplementing these two books is that a number of films which Mr Blesh was apparently unable to see have meanwhile become available; while Keaton's modesty made his own book disappointingly weak in documentation about his pictures.

In a number of ways the films of Buster Keaton are unusually delightful to write about, and unusually difficult. For a start there is no obvious progression and development to be traced through them. The early days are somewhat tentative, it is true, but he arrived in the cinema with a marvellous and intact apparatus. *The Boat* is as perfect and mature in its way as *The General*; and Keaton's second silent feature is in no respect less accomplished than his last ones. And because Keaton was a genius (whatever sense you give to the term) and because his creation has a mystic quality detached from his private and personal being, elaborate Freudian interpretations of his creative processes seem as irrelevant as are ordinary, formal aesthetic criteria to an artist who was innocent of practically any considered artistic principle beyond 'getting a laugh without being too ridiculous,' and yet whose work turned out to be pure art and pure poetry. The best approach, it has seemed to me, has been to follow out his career, as he tried to do a job, and as he mastered the elements of his craft. This book does not pretend to be more than description and idolatry.

2: Vaudeville

'From the beginning,' he wrote, 'I was surrounded by interesting people who loved fun and knew how to create it.' He was born on 4 October 1895. His father was Joseph Hollie Keaton (1867–1946), the son of a miller, who had staked a claim in the Oklahoma Land Rush of 1889, which he handed over to his parents when he joined a medicine show. Keaton's mother, *née* Myra Edith Cutler (1877–1955), met her future husband when he was working in the Cutler-Bryant Medicine Show, of which her father was co-proprietor. When their eldest son was born, the Keatons were still working with travelling medicine shows; and he was delivered in a theatrical lodging-house in Piqua, Kansas, where they were appearing with the Mohawk Medicine Company. They continued to tour with fit-up roadshows (in Dr Hill's California Concert Company they were with Houdini and his wife) until 1899, when they broke modestly into vaudeville at Huhin's Museum, New York.

The Keatons seemed peculiarly prone to accidents. Pregnant with young Joseph Francis, his mother was thrown from a buggy, got tangled in a storm-felled tent, and fell from the stage during a performance. Throughout the child's infancy and youth the family seemed constantly to be involved in hotel or theatre fires. Before the age of one he was practically suffocated in the costume trunk in which he slept while the parents were working. He was given the name of 'Buster' by Harry Houdini after he had successfully fallen down a flight of stairs in a theatrical boarding-house, at the

Buster as one of The Three Keatons, *c.* 1900 →

age of six months. In later years he was rather sad that people tended to disbelieve his account of the most adventurous day of his childhood, in Kansas, in July 1898, when in quick succession he tangled his fingers in the cogs of a wringer, brained himself with a rock which he had thrown up to dislodge a peach from a tree, and was sucked by a cyclone out of his hotel room and carried a block or more to be deposited in the street, unharmed. The striking thing about all these accidents is the way in which they seem directly to prefigure incidents in Keaton films.

Buster appears to have made his first accidental appearance on the stage when he crawled on in the course of his father's act around July 1896; but it was not until 1898 that he officially joined the family act, apparently because of his mother's reluctance (in all the circumstances, not unreasonable) to let him out of her sight. His first role in the act (which now changed its billing from The Two Keatons to The Three Keatons) was to appear as a miniature version of his father, wearing an identical comic Irish get-up, 'with a fright wig, slugger whiskers, fancy vest and over-size pants.' After the Keatons left medicine shows for vaudeville, Buster was unwillingly kept off the stage for a year or so by the Gerry Society, which was active in the major towns to prevent exploitation of children. In October 1900, however, William Dockstader encouraged the Keatons to put the child back in the act, at his Wonderland Theatre in Wilmington.

The elder Keaton's speciality was acrobatic comedy (his cele-brated high kick may be seen in *Our Hospitality*; it is said that he could reach a height of ten feet with a hitch kick). Father and son were able to turn nursery horse-play into an improvisational knockabout act, centred on the idea of a high-spirited child and his harassed parent. Buster hurled things at his father's head, stepped on him when he had tripped him up, and swatted him with fly-swatters and brooms. In retaliation the father swung the child about the stage by means of a suitcase handle strapped to his back, and slid him all about the floor as 'The Human Mop.' (There is a curious similarity here to the debut of Joe Grimaldi, whose first stage appearances, at under two years old, were rough-housing with his clown father. Young Joe was on one occasion accidentally thrown into the audience; Buster's father deliberately threw him at some rowdy college boys in the front row of Poli's, New Haven, one day in 1903.)

It is clear that even by the age of five Buster had learned a remarkable repertory of falls and stage acrobatics. 'Oddly enough, I cannot remember Pop teaching me anything. I just watched what he did, then did the same thing. I could take crazy falls without hurting myself simply because I had learnt the trick so early in life that body control became pure instinct with me. If I never broke a bone on the stage it is because I always avoided taking the impact of a fall on the back of my head, the base of my spine, on my elbows or my knees. That's how bones are broken. You also bruise only if you do not know as I do which muscles to tighten, which ones to relax.' He acquired other outlandish skills which he was later to make relevant to his art: 'I was just a harebrained kid that was raised backstage. He tries everything as he grows up. If there is a wire-walker this week, well he tries walking a wire when nobody's looking. If there's a juggler, he tries to juggle—he tries to do acrobatics—there's nothing he don't try. He tries to be a ventriloquist—he tries to be a juggling fool, a magician—Harry Houdini. I tried to get out of handcuffs and strait jackets.'

He developed a precocious instinct for comic invention and improvisation, a shrewd sense of what made people laugh. It was at this stage that he developed his characteristically impassive style. 'I learned as a kid growing up with an audience that I just had to be that type of comedian—if I laughed at what I did, the audience didn't. . . . The more serious I turned the bigger laugh I could get. So at the time I went into pictures, that was automatic —I didn't even know I was doing it.' He developed precision in timing his comedy. 'The old man would kick me a hell of a wallop. . . . Now a strange thing developed. If I yelled ouch—no laughs. If I deadpanned it and didn't yell—no laughs. "What goes?" I asked, "isn't a kick funny?" "Not by itself it ain't," said Joe. So he gives me a little lesson: I wait five seconds—count up to ten slow—grab the seat of my pants, holler bloody murder, and the audience is rolling in the aisles. I don't know what the thunder they figured. Maybe that it took five seconds for a kick to travel from my fanny to my brain. Actually I guess, it was The Slow Thinker. Audiences love The Slow Thinker.'

His comic ability as a child must have been phenomenal. By the time he was five or six (and the Gerry Society had been put off the scent by misrepresenting his age as seven) he was being billed as 'BUSTER, assisted by Joe and Myra Keaton.' 'The reason managers approved of my being featured was because I was unique, being at that time the only little hell-raising Huck Finn type boy in vaudeville. The parents of the others presented their boys as cute and charming Little Lord Fauntleroys. . . .' One of the most persuasive evidences of his talent at the time is the rumour prevalent about 1902 and 1903 that he was not a child at all, but a clever midget. It is important to realise that for something like fifteen years before he entered films he was already a minor star in his own right.

Rudi Blesh has tried to re-create some impression of the Keaton act: 'It was never the same way twice; it threw away its clichés before they could crystallise. People came back day after day to see what would happen next, just as they followed the cartoon strips, *Happy Hooligan*, *The Yellow Kid* and *The Katzenjammers*. Monday might be twenty minutes of up-tempo mayhem relieved by 'My Gal Sal' on alto sax—practical joke and counter-joke, slips, tumbles, trips, slides, and the unbelievable comic falls. Tuesday might develop into one long comic-story routine all in off-the-cuff pantomime and not a word spoken. Wednesday would perhaps unfold as recitation time, with merciless parodies of Bernhardt, Eva Tanguay or Sothern and Marlowe's Romeo and Juliet, with the balcony and Buster falling on Joe. Thursday might be devoted to one long outrageous burlesque of some popular melodrama. Or all these things and more might be cross-stitched into a Keaton sampler of the modes of madness.' Nightly improvisation made invention a habit with the young Keaton. 'We never bothered to do the same routines twice in a row. We found it much more fun to surprise one another by pulling any crazy, wild stunt that came into our heads.'

No other period and no other theatre could have provided Keaton with a more favourable climate in which to develop the faculties, skills and attitudes which he was later to apply to a new medium. Vaudeville (and, in England, variety) was a unique theatrical phenomenon which rose and declined with a particular epoch and a particular audience. It was popular, lawless (artistically speaking) and opulent. In its origins it offered variety and colour to people whose ordinary lives were monotonous and drab. It could juxtapose without embarrassment Bernhardt or Pavlova and W. C. Fields, robots, performing dogs, *poses plastiques* or the wrestling cheese which Keaton recalled later as one of William Hammerstein's more exceptional attractions. The audience did not mind what they saw so long as whatever it was it was extraordinary. (Keaton also recalled another Hammerstein attraction, The Cherry Sisters, who were so extraordinarily bad that a screen was put in front of them, and the audience supplied with rotten vegetables and other missiles.) In matter of quality the audience was nevertheless often discriminating, demanding and censorious. In consequence this essentially popular art achieved—in artists like Fields or Marie Lloyd or Hetty King or Elsie Janis or Albert Chevalier or Gus Elen or George M. Cohan—a sophistication and polish to equal any other theatrical tradition whatsoever. As the nineteenth century ended, the heightened sophistication of the entertainment had attracted more sophisticated audiences, and in turn greater discrimination and still higher standards of performance.

What vaudeville had to teach its practitioners was a discipline and method. The vaudeville act had to put itself over to a critical and not very patient audience, in a strictly limited time—it could be sixteen minutes or it could be eight—and against relentless competition and without benefit of a favourable context (a dramatic monologuist might be sandwiched between knockabout comics and performing seals).

The good vaudeville act learned the secret of infallible attack. It learned structure, the need to give an act a clear and effective beginning, middle and end. It had to control every kind of audience, to anticipate and profit by the audience's responses, gaining momentum from the audience as a judo fighter does from his opponent. It was an audience keenly alert to falsehood. If a vaudeville performer set out to create a character—and character comedy was the basis of all the best of vaudeville: W. C. Fields, for instance, was a great juggler, but it was as a character comic that he was established—the character had to be recognisably consistent and truthful, even in its absurdity. To the end of his life one of Keaton's most important criteria of comedy and comic characterisation was the condition that it should not be 'ridiculous' (he liked the Marx Brothers, for instance, only 'when they don't get ridiculous')—by which he stressed the need for comedy to observe its own laws of dramatic and psychological integrity.

Vaudeville acts were rarely scripted in advance or written down. Generally they were developed in performance, and perfected against the reactions of an audience. A special characteristic of vaudeville and music-hall was the possibility of touring an act for many years, refining it the whole time; which is how performers like Fields or Hetty King or Gus Elen were able to achieve such perfection of technique and timing. Keaton described a typical instance of the genesis and polishing of a bit of stage business: ' . . . Then I found that knothole in the floor at Columbus. Stopped and looked at it with that alley broom in my hand and walked away. Walked back and looked at it again, jabbed at it with the broom handle and missed. Gave up and walked away again. Just then Joe started his recitation and needed a noise obbligato. So I walk over and really go to work on it. Jab and miss, jab and miss. Get into every crazy position—even on my head—to aim better but still miss. Sounded like the Light Brigade; no one could hear a word Joe was saying. He picked up the gag, stopping and starting over, doing the slow burn.'

'Then he begins to really wonder, "What the hell *is* that over there?" walks over and I point at the hole as serious as if God only knows what's down in there. I keep missing. So I get sore, take off

Vaudevillian and film actor

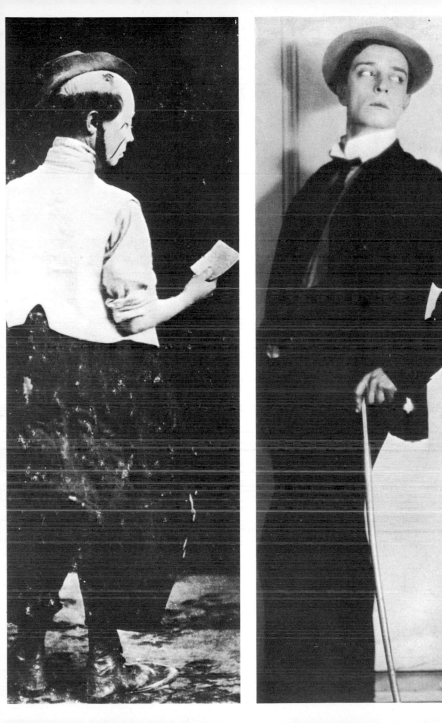

my coat, roll up my sleeves, spit on my palms, take the broom in both hands, sight down the handle, take aim—Joe bending over watching me—shake my head, line it up again, take a fresh aim. More of a production, for Chrissake, than Palmer lining up a thirty-foot putt. Finally I let fly. Hit the hole at last; then the broom goes in up to the bristles, and I go smack on my face with my feet up in the air. A beautiful fall. After all that build-up the audience is absolutely killing itself. All over a hole in the floor.'

The gag was crowned by having the broom appear to stick down the hole, whereupon the Keatons would pull and tug at it until it suddenly came loose, catapulting them into 'a clubhouse sandwich pratfall.' After Columbus, they always bored a hole in the stage of any theatre they performed in; and fragments of the routine appear from time to time in Keaton's films, most notably in *The Playhouse*.

Working out routines in this way, the vaudeville performer—who was, of course, his own producer, director and designer—acquired an infallible capacity for the solution of stage problems. A line or a gag or a detail had to be prepared and placed and projected in the most effective manner possible. Either empirically or through an instinct born of years of practice, the performer generally found the most exact and just solution to any question of staging. Anyone who can remember even the weariest latter-day music-hall bills of twenty years or so ago, will recall how even the least distinguished performers on them still often achieved exemplary theatrical standards of technical presentation. Buster Keaton, knowing no way of life but vaudeville, absorbed all the lessons it had to teach until they became second nature to him.

The Keaton act broke up in February 1917, after several years during which drinking and disappointment had made Joe Keaton an increasingly difficult partner. After he had threatened physical violence upon the person of Martin Beck—an unpopular but influential impresario much identified with the management trusts of the early years of the century—the act began to get worse and worse bookings. Joe's drinking also became worse and the rough-house act became positively dangerous. One night, between engagements, while Joe Keaton was in a saloon, Buster and his mother walked out.

It is further evidence of Buster's high personal prestige at the age of twenty-one that he was immediately signed up by the Shuberts for their *Passing Show of 1917* at the Winter Garden, at a salary of $250 a week, $300 on tour. But he never even began rehearsals. Instead he went into the movies at a salary of $40 a week.

3: The Arbuckle Period

'. . . I was walking down Broadway—down along Eighth or some place—and I met an old vaudevillian* and he was with Roscoe (Fatty) Arbuckle and he told me that he took his make-up off for a while and was going to try running a motion picture company for Joe Schenck who was producing pictures with Norma Talmadge and Constance Talmadge at the Colony Studio on 48th Street in New York, and that he had just signed Arbuckle from Sennett. And Roscoe asked me if I had ever been in a motion picture, and I said no I hadn't even been in a studio. And he said, well come on down to the studio Monday and do a scene with me or two and see how you like it. I said, well rehearsals don't start for another week or so, so I'll be there. I went down there and I worked in it. . . .'

The casualness of it is outrageous. Behind it, however, there must have been a powerful instinct of predestination. Even Keaton, who was quite truthfully 'not very bothered about money', could not chuck up a plum theatre job for less than a quarter of the salary without some sort of vision of the future. As early as 1913 William Randolph Hearst had tried to interest the Keaton family in making a series of film comedies based on a popular comic strip, *Bringing Up Father*; but the conservative Keaton Senior had rejected the idea. Even at that time Buster Keaton seems to have

---

* Lou Anger, formerly a 'Dutch' comic, who later became Keaton's own manager.

Roscoe Arbuckle

Arbuckle and Keaton with (*left*) Alice Lake and (*right*) Viola Dana

been disappointed. In 1917, Keaton's agent, however he may have regretted his personal loss, clearly felt that the decision was correct: 'Learn everything you can about that business, Buster, the hell with the money. Movies are the coming thing, believe me.'

The advice, it seems, was superfluous. From the first day he set foot in the Arbuckle Studios, Keaton's mechanical curiosity demanded to know everything there was to know about the techniques of film-making. 'He lived in the camera,' Arbuckle later recalled; while in later years Keaton insisted that whereas his father taught him all he knew about stage comedy, it was Arbuckle who was his master in pictures. 'But not from an audience stand-point—I learned that for myself and from my father, 'cause I had all that experience. See by the time I'm 21 years old, I'm a vet.'

Historical and critical assessments of Roscoe Arbuckle are still to a remarkable degree clouded by the disagreeable circumstances of the manslaughter case in which he was involved in 1921–22. In the course of a bootleg party in Arbuckle's suite in a San Francisco hotel, a Hollywood bit player named Virginia Rappe was taken ill and subsequently died. After three trials the prosecution case disintegrated, and Arbuckle was acquitted of any involvement in her death. But as one of Arbuckle's lawyers said at the time, his weight condemned him. The women's clubs of America were not to be cheated of the horror fantasies they had woven around the idea of the laughing, leering fat beast and the helpless young beauty. (The evidence in fact all indicated that Rappe was very little better than she should have been.) Arbuckle was henceforth no longer allowed to work as an actor in films, and Zukor was forced by public opinion to withdraw all the comedian's pictures from circulation. In consequence comparatively little of his considerable output of shorts seems to have survived. Moreover our judgement of it is still in some inescapable manner coloured by a half-conscious inherited memory of the associations of the Rappe case. Practically every modern writer finds himself qualifying grudging praise of Arbuckle's work with the word 'repellent'; and this reaction lies deeper than modern squeamishness over the exploitation of comic possibilities in physical abnormality. Somehow we still feel the chill of orgy and sudden death. We no longer see the fat, jolly, baby-faced young man whom his contemporaries loved exceedingly until they turned upon him. It is fortunate for posterity that Keaton did not accept Arbuckle's invitation to his Labour Day party.

Keaton, who knew Arbuckle perhaps as well as anyone, loved him as a man and deeply admired him as a clown. He was, he said, 'that rarity, a truly jolly fat man. He had no meanness, malice or jealousy in him.' Certainly, very few actors directing their own company would have permitted a supporting player to become co-star and in the end to overshadow them, as Arbuckle cheerfully allowed Keaton to do. To the end of his days, Keaton kept a large portrait photograph of Roscoe on his wall.

As a performer Arbuckle alternated frenetic activity—running, leaping and arm-waving are always comical in a fat man—with a rather cool and deft management of more detailed knockabout. He took very good falls. He had a phenomenal dexterity. He was known to be able to shy custard pies or other missiles in two directions at the same time and with perfect accuracy. In *The Butcher Boy* he tosses a lethal butcher's knife over his shoulder so that it falls with nice precision, point downwards in a chopping-block behind his back. He could roll a cigarette in an instant with one hand only. He had a weakness for putting on female costume, which (if we can, again, detach ourselves from modern nerviness about transvestism) often produced very funny effects. He looked beautifully grotesque skipping coyly up a long road in a ballooning Mary Pickford get-up.

As a film-maker (and from Keystone days on he wrote and directed his own films) he remained essentially a primitive. Perhaps he had learned his film-craft too early. Born in 1887, he seems to have gone into pictures at least as early as 1909, after years of working as a comic and singer in fit-ups which toured backwoods pioneer camps, and later in vaudeville. Despite the immense popularity which he started to earn with Sennett, the films he was making at the time Keaton joined him were crude in the extreme by comparison with the films which Chaplin, for instance, was making at the same period. It seems practically inconceivable that *The Butcher Boy* was released three months after *Easy Street* and only three months before *The Immigrant*.

Arbuckle's own character was never developed to any degree: he was simply a working-class boy who did funny things, who was lovesick for some girl and who generally won her in the face of a wily rival. The character, the context and the story were never interwoven in any sophisticated way. The setting of the Arbuckle films was very much a Casey's Court world of wooden fences, motor cars, fire hoses, general stores, bakeries, torn trousers, angry old women and dogs, flirty housemaids, galloping policemen, hot stoves to be sat on and custard pies to be pushed or thrown into other people's faces.

Starting with a given setting (a garage, bakery, hospital, music hall or Coney Island) the object was simply to fit in as many elementary comic-strip gags as possible, and to find the greatest number of excuses for each character to assault the others, and as large a variety of weapons as possible with which to do it. The cavorting and grimacing of Arbuckle's brother-in-law, Al St John —one of the least talented and least lovable slapstick comedians— suited the formula ideally. The films had no structure to speak of. The two-reelers tended to fall into two distinct parts. Generally speaking the comic possibilities of the main setting were exhausted by the end of the first reel, so quite arbitrarily the film would start up again, for the second reel, with a new scene and a new scheme of activity.

It is not easy to assess the exact impact of Keaton upon Arbuckle's Comicque Studios, or the stages of his development during the two years or so that he was associated with them, because of the lack of firm record, and the confusion and corruption of the copies that have survived. There is even a little uncertainty about how many films Keaton made with Arbuckle. Certainly there were fourteen (of which, remarkably, more than half survive), but there could have been more. Most Keaton filmographies list *A Country Hero*, although this title was not released until a whole year after the last certain Keaton-Arbuckle short, *The Garage*, and long after Keaton had left to establish his own studio. A few filmographies list as the second Arbuckle-Keaton *A Reckless Romeo*; but no film of this title was ever registered with the Library of Congress; and it may refer to the reel which now appears as the second part of *The Butcher Boy* (with the first part of which it has no explicable narrative or continuity connection), involving Arbuckle and St John in female disguise, with Buster assisting them to arrange the heroine's elopement with Fatty from a girl's finishing-school.

There are further confusions. Copies have been reclaimed from foreign sources, or in other ways have lost their original titles, so that there is a possibility of confusion between *Oh Doctor* and *Goodnight Nurse*; between *Out West* and *A Desert Hero* and between *The Hayseed* and *A Country Hero* (if this was in fact a Keaton film). Nor do release dates, which are easily established, necessarily correspond to the order in which the films were made.

Only as and if new film material comes to light are such problems likely to be resolved.

Two things however are certain. *The Butcher Boy* marked Keaton's debut on the screen; and the Arbuckle series show a very marked sophistication in form, in content and in style during the two years in which Keaton worked at the Comicque Studios. Characteristic of this sophistication is the increasing introduction of gags in a recognisable Keaton taste.

The Butcher Boy is set in a village store, with all the predictable vaudeville-slapstick-comic-strip gags about the pretty cashier, the irascible old proprietor, the overhead cash railway, the difficult customers. There is a coffee-mill powered by a treadmill worked by a dog, and comic notices on the wall such as 'Fresh sausages made every month.' Fatty is the butcher boy; he emerges from the refrigerator in a huge fur coat and launches into a series of dexterous gags with meat, sausages, knives and a pair of scales.

Keaton's entry on this scene is momentous, for this, before our very eyes, is the record of his first day in a film studio, his first appearance before the motion-picture camera. The scene was shot in one take. What we see is the perfect vaudevillian at work, his uncanny instinct already scaling and directing his performance to the viewpoint of the camera. He introduces a style in direct contrast to his fellow performers—the style which he was to develop and refine. While their movements are extravagant and over-emphatic, excessive, he is quiet, controlled, unhurried, economical, accurate. His solitary calm already rivets attention.

He enters by a door on the right of the screen, and at first we see only his back. He is a rube, wearing baggy overalls and big slapshoes and, already, the familiar flat hat. Over his arm he carries a tin can with a wire handle. As he turns we perceive that though the figure is small and stumpy, the face—unsmiling and totally dignified—is handsome: the taut, smooth skin, the large, lidded eyes, the straight nose which continues in a direct line from the forehead, the neat firm mouth are all simplified to a classical beauty like a Cocteau drawing. He was twenty-one.

The Keatons' stage act always involved a selection of brooms ('thirteen or fourteen,' Keaton invariably recalled, with quaintly precise uncertainty) which served a variety of comic purposes. By chance a barrel just inside the door of the general store of *The Butcher Boy* contains thirteen or fourteen brooms. Buster selects one, tries the bristles for strength and plucks it like a chicken. He picks out a better one and then tosses the rejects back into the barrel with satisfying accuracy of aim.

He suddenly notices a pool of molasses which has dripped on to the floor from the tap of a barrel. Furtively he sticks his shoe into it and then wipes the molasses off his sole with his finger, which he licks. A little bolder, he wipes the tap itself with his finger.

Arriving at Fatty's counter, he pulls a quarter piece out of his pocket. There is a brief but telling demonstration of his stage-craft in the way that he tosses the coin in the air and kisses it before dropping it into his tin. This bit of business unemphatically but completely focuses our attention upon the coin which is central to the gag that is to follow. He slaps the can down on the counter, startling Fatty. While Fatty is filling the can with molasses, Buster shyly 'helps' some irritated old men with their game of checkers. Fatty hands over the filled tin and holds out his hand for payment. Buster points innocently to the tin. Unable to retrieve the coin from the bottom of the molasses with his yardstick, Fatty pours the molasses into Buster's hat while Buster is looking the other way. Buster puts on his hat. Very gradually he realises that something is amiss. With mounting anxiety he tries to pull off the hat, in the process dropping the tin and spilling the molasses in a pool on the floor. Fatty tries to pull off the hat and Buster steps into the molasses. The initial slow recognition of his predicament has now grown into panic. Fatty's efforts to help him become more violent, and end, first with a kettle of boiling water poured over Buster's feet, both of which are now glued fast; and finally with a mighty kick which lands Buster through the door and somersaulting down the store steps into the road outside. The indignant Buster re-enters the shop just in time to receive a flour sack in the face. (He never forgot this particular gag: his varying descriptions and admiration of the force and accuracy of Arbuckle's aim appear in all his biographies and interviews.) He lunges at Al St John with a broom, but succeeds only in landing himself in a fine pratfall. The first half of the picture ends with a great mêlée of flour-flinging.

In the second half of the film Keaton is subordinated to the travesty antics of Arbuckle and St John, though he has a memorable moment when, threatened by an angry schoolmistress armed with a shot-gun, he does a beautiful back fall to land in a reclining hands-up pose.

This first film appearance of Keaton's is worth detailing at length for it gives us some idea of the equipment he brought from vaudeville to the cinema. It shows him already, in his first day's work in pictures, imposing his own rhythm, his own sense of timing and construction of a gag upon a team given to much less disciplined modes of comedy creation.

The Butcher Boy and the succeeding films, the alleged *A Reckless Romeo* and *Rough House*, neither of which now survive, were made at the Colony Studios on 48th Street. Three more films were made in New York, at studios on 174th Street. Of these *His Wedding Night* has disappeared; while *Oh Doctor* cannot with certainty be distinguished from *Goodnight Nurse*—though whichever of the two is the survivor is fairly crude and, with jokes about lady lunatics and crazy chases in a park-like garden, gives little scope to Keaton's personal comedy style. In *Coney Island* Keaton has certainly compromised to the prevailing ways of the Comicque Company. He cheerfully gags and laughs and doubles his roles as a visitor to Coney Island and a comic cop. There is all the same some spectacular knockabout, much of it improvised against the background of 1917 Coney Island.

In an interview in the late fifties, Keaton recalled a gag in which he and Arbuckle were shot out of a water-chute. 'Roscoe takes the girl on the "shoot-the-shoots." And when that boat first hits the water it kind of skids past. But when she hits the second time she has a strong lift to the bow. "Well," Roscoe says, "that'll throw anyone out of the boat that wants to get thrown." See; if you don't

Coney Island

hang on in other words. Says "All right," says "put the girl's clothes on Keaton and we'll try it." So I doubled for the girl. What we did was, 'stead of sitting on the seat we crouched on it, just held underneath to hold on. He took me by the hand and we came down that chute, and when that boat hit the first lift we lifted with it. The camera was back about a hundred feet to photograph that, and we went out of the top of the frame. That's how far it threw us. Me being the lightest and holding Arbuckle's hand he threw me so that I went just that much higher than he did. When I came down I hit him on the back of his neck as he hit the water. Nobody was hurt though. . . . In those early films, oh, we got our bumps and bruises and sometimes got laid up for a couple of days; but seldom anything serious.' A scene of confusion in the changing-room of a swimming-pool looks forward to the pool sequence of *The Cameraman.*

After *Coney Island* the Arbuckle studio was moved to Long Beach, California, and celebrated with a film which exploited their exciting new locations—*Out West.* This, along with *The Bell Boy, Moonshine* and (depending on the identification of *Oh Doctor*) *Goodnight Nurse* have all now vanished; but the succeeding five films which Keaton made before leaving Arbuckle have survived.

Out West

The Cook is very much Arbuckle's film. In the characteristic way, it falls into two distinct halves. In the first reel Arbuckle is involved between a hen-pecking family and an attractive cook-housemaid (Alice Lake), and finishes up in a wild slapstick chase with Buster, who seems to be the gardener, and Al St John. The second part of the film introduces some nonsense with thieves and comic policemen. As one of the cops, Keaton manages to get ridiculously caught atop a fence in the course of the chase. It is in this film, however, that we have the first clear and sustained evidence of an identifiable Keaton comedy style. There is his favourite joke of disproportion in Arbuckle's attempts to put out a fire with water brought in a teacup. Absent-mindedly returning to the fire with the second cupful, Arbuckle, with very Keatonian abstraction, drinks it on the way. Other gags which smack more of Keaton's style than any precedents in the Arbuckle films are the mechanical ingenuity of using an electric fan to chop vegetables;

Fatty's trick of laying the table by setting down a bundled-up cloth which unwraps to reveal perfect place settings; and the blood-curdling bit of camera trickery by which Al St John is made to catch in his teeth a knife thrown by an uncharacteristically murderous Keaton. Keaton's own business is fairly restricted again, though it includes a splendid entrance on a bicycle from which he is violently snatched by a taut clothes-line.

If we suppose that by this time, and in particular in *The Cook*, Keaton was taking a hand in the invention of comedy material for the Arbuckle films, one scene becomes especially intriguing. Sitting at the dinner-table with his disapproving female relatives, Fatty spears two rolls on the end of forks, and makes the miniature booted legs thus formed perform a little dance. It is a curious thought that it may have been Keaton who thought up this gag, seven years before Chaplin made it his own and famous in *The Gold Rush*. (One must not, of course, discount the possibility that it was Arbuckle who had picked up the gag from Chaplin, long before it was used in any film, during their days together with Sennett.)

After *The Cook*, Keaton joined the army and served the last months of the war and the early part of 1919 with the 40th Infantry. On demobilisation he was offered a thousand-dollar-a-week contract by Jack L. Warner; but again he settled for a quarter the salary to stay with Arbuckle, who by this time had moved to new studios in Alvarado Street. Again the record is rather misty. Keaton, whose memory was generally extremely reliable in the matter of his own films, insisted in every interview and in his autobiography, 'I only made two more two reelers with Roscoe.' Yet *four* films were released after his military service and after a pause in Arbuckle Comicque releases which corresponds to the period of his absence. *The Cook* was released in August 1918; *A Desert Hero, Back Stage, The Hayseed* and *The Garage* came out in June, August, October and December 1919. (The mysterious *A Country Hero* was released exactly a year after the last of these.) Of these films all but the first were released under a new arrangement which Joseph M. Schenck had negotiated with Famous

The Garage

Players-Lasky and Paramount. It seems unlikely that Arbuckle would hold up the release of two films for practically a year, but not impossible if, for instance, he had been negotiating and preparing productions for the new releasing arrangement. With Arbuckle, Schenck and Keaton all dead and the old studio records no longer available, it is difficult to confirm Keaton's assertion or to be sure of the order in which the films were made. What is certain, however, is that *A Desert Hero* and *The Hayseed* are in quite a different style from *Back Stage* and *The Garage*; and that *Back Stage* and *The Garage* not only have certain direct correspondences to individual Keaton shorts (*Playhouse*, *The Blacksmith*) in content, but in composition and style are very much closer to the Keaton shorts than to any of the work with Arbuckle that preceded them.

In *A Desert Hero* Keaton is a dude in a top hat and frock-coat, in a wild west saloon, and his adventures with Al St John as a

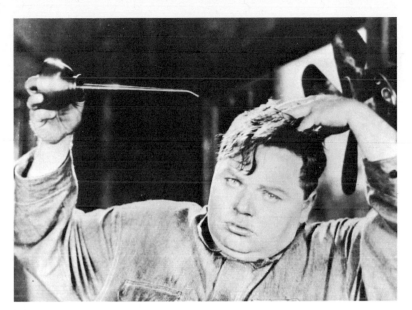

The Garage

hold-up man, and Fatty as a sort of hobo, are pretty arbitrary. Keaton's own business is mostly uncharacteristic (apart from a nice moment of blank astonishment when St John simply breaks the gun with which Buster is holding him up). Some bits of business—the whisky glass used as an eye-bath, the *boutonnière* which he drops down a trapdoor on top of a card-cheat whom he has just shot dead—are much more reminiscent of Chaplin than of Keaton himself. Fatty however has a long and ingenious sequence with a train which looks distinctly like a Keaton invention. Riding on the roof of a train, Fatty is soaked by the boiler feed before dropping through a trap in the roof on to some gamblers in the carriage below. They give chase, along the top of the train. Dismounting from the front of the train, Fatty nonchalantly strikes a match on the side of the moving train, before remounting on the last carriage while his pursuers are still running towards the front. When they turn around and start running back, Fatty releases the brake-van and waves good-bye as the train and pursuers retreat into the distance. As he is sitting down to a peaceful lunch, however, the train backs again, picks up the brake-van. Fatty is caught and ejected into the desert. The sequence, it will be seen, contains elements all of which were later incorporated into various Keaton railway sequences.

The Hayseed is only slightly better constructed than this generally muddled film. Fatty works in the village general store and delivers the mail. Buster, as a general help, sees the crooked sheriff stealing a registered letter, and so is subsequently able to clear Fatty when he is charged with the theft. Fatty's business is loose and charmless; but this time Buster himself has some Keatonish jokes. When the film opens he is discovered oiling the joints of Fatty's horse. Later there is a characteristically geometrical piece of acrobatics when Buster escapes from a roof-top on the end of a falling ladder, which arcs down—like the pole-gate in *Sherlock Junior*—to deposit him accurately in Fatty's buggy. There is, too, a simple technical trick which makes use of reversing the film, as had already been done with the knife-in-mouth gag in *The Cook*. Here the device is used with rather less sophistication. Buster drives up in the buggy, and is ordered to take it back to the stable. He does so, in reverse motion.

Back Stage marks a complete revolution in style. From start to finish it has all the marks of a Buster Keaton two-reeler, in structure and in gags. For the first time there is the characteristic Keaton opening, which he was to use again and again, in which what first appears to our view is an illusion and a deception, the facts of the situation being gradually revealed to us. Keaton is discovered in bed in his bedroom. Then the entire bedroom disintegrates: for it is a scene in the theatre and is being struck. Outside the theatre Fatty (with interference from an inquisitive child who ends up pasted to the wall) is sticking up a bill, which is used for another favourite Keaton gag—the partially obscured message (cf. the Julian Eltinge joke in *Seven Chances* and the confusion of pier numbers in *The Navigator*). The poster Fatty puts up reads:

GERTRUDE MC SKINNY
FAMOUS STAR WHO WILL
PLAY
THE LITTLE LA UNDRESS
FIRST TIME HERE
TOMORROW AT 2 p.m.

When a flat is leaned against the left-hand side of the poster, the legend becomes much more appealing.

Back in the theatre there is another charming little gag on the same lines as the favourite deception-opening. Buster keeps disappearing down a flight of stairs and reappearing. Then we discover that what looks like the solid banister is really a flat on its side; and he is merely going down on his knees on the level floor behind it, in order to nail something to the ground. The theatre also contains a typical piece of Keaton engineering: a star on a system of pulleys and wires which can be moved from one dressing-room door to another at will.

In *Back Stage*, too, one of Keaton's favourite and most famous and spectacular gags appears in prototype. In the course of the performance Fatty and Buster, having already performed a delicious Grecian *pas de deux*, in the Isadora manner, and with Keaton as the lady, appear in a prop car, as passenger and chauffeur respectively. When Buster entangles the car with the scenery, a huge prop house-side falls down on Fatty, its open upper window neatly clearing him as it falls to the ground around him. This gag was to be developed through *One Week* to its perfection in *Steamboat Bill Jr.*

Practically for the first time in the Arbuckle series of two-reelers, *Back Stage* has a reasonably defined plot: the worsting of the strong man with whose ill-used and bullied daughter (?) Fatty is in love. The climax of the film is when Keaton, on a trapeze, swings right across the theatre from the stage to the dress circle to snatch up the villain and bring him back in his arms to the stage. In the scene that follows, Buster launches a frenzied attack on the villain, hurling himself at him with tremendous verve and insistence, feet first, head first, any way that will turn him into an effective missile.

Back Stage, like *The Garage*, released in December 1919 and almost certainly the last Keaton-Arbuckle collaboration, shows the whole style of the Comicque company refined and restrained until it approximates to Keaton's own preferred tempo and manner. Significantly Al St John was absent from these two films, and Arbuckle had adapted himself much more to Keaton's way of working. It is interesting to note how much more cleverly Arbuckle in *The Garage* manages a Keaton-style gag than he did, say, in *The Cook* or *A Desert Hero*. The hose has a leak, so Arbuckle sits on it. As he does so a tram runs over another part of the hose, puncturing it in two places. Even his generous surface cannot cope with this. A year earlier this predicament would have been the signal for a good deal of arm-waving and mugging towards the camera. Now he simply looks at the new fountains with resigned bewilderment.

Even in the frank slapstick of the opening, a terrible mêlée of hoses and oil and sumps and collapsing cars, a more restrained Arbuckle is at once a better partner for Keaton and a funnier comedian. Again we see the characteristic Keaton gags developing richly. Finding himself trouserless, Buster cuts the kilt off a life-size poster portrait of Harry Lauder, and is only detected by a policeman when he gets too smart, does a highland fling and spins right round. There is a prototype mechanised dwelling in the arrangement he and Fatty have for a quick getaway in case of fire (the garage of the title also serves as a fire station). An alarm system not only gets them out of bed, but whips off the night-shirts which they wear over their street clothes. The reverse film gag is now used with immeasurably greater sophistication. The picture ends with a fire (as tidily plotted as anything in Keaton's mature films). The heroine (Molly Malone) leaps out of an upper window into the firemen's sheet; and bounces straight back up again and on to some overhead telephone wires. At that point the dinner whistle blows, and all the firemen go off duty, leaving Fatty and Buster to rescue the first, but by no means the last, Keaton heroine to be rough-housed as no other comedy heroines ever were.

4: The Keaton Studio

At the end of 1919 Joseph Schenck organised a new company to produce a series of shorts in which Keaton would star. The former Chaplin studios were acquired and reopened in January 1920 as the Keaton Studio. The exact financial set-up of the company is uncertain, and perhaps at this stage not especially significant. From *One Week* (September 1920) to *The Goat* (May 1921) Keaton films were registered as Metro releases, produced by Joseph M. Schenck. *The Playhouse* (October 1921) was simply registered as a First National release. From *The Boat* (November 1921) to *The Blacksmith* (July 1922) films were registered as productions of the Comique Film Co. Inc. (as distinct from Arbuckle's Comicque Studio), presented by Joseph M. Schenck and released through First National. From *The Frozen North* (August 1922) to *The Love Nest* (March 1923) they were in the name of Buster Keaton Productions Inc., presented by Joseph M. Schenck and released by Associated First National.

The important thing about the business set-up of the Keaton Studio, however, is that throughout the period—and right up to *Steamboat Bill Jr.*, after which Keaton was absorbed into the M-G-M organisation—Schenck relieved the comedian of all the business worries of the organisation, simply guaranteeing for him a complete freedom of working conditions. Keaton's contract with the company 'gave me $1,000 a week, plus 25 per cent of the profits my pictures made.'

The new Keaton Studio was, it seems, ready ahead of schedule; and Keaton found himself with four weeks to spare before he began work on a feature-length comedy for Metro, which Schenck had arranged for him, presumably to tide over any gap between the parting from Arbuckle and the commencement of production at his own studios. Keaton used the time to make his first starring short, *The High Sign*. Unaccountably he always regarded this as a failure; and in fact shelved it for more than a year, only releasing it in April 1921, after *The Saphead* and six further two-reelers had firmly established him as a major star.

It is not easy to account for his distaste. Even this first film shows a marked advance on the Arbuckle series and is fairly rich in Keaton gags, recognisably of the great period. 'Our hero came from NOWHERE. He wasn't going ANYWHERE and got kicked out of SOMEWHERE.' He answers an advertisement for a shooting-gallery attendant, manages by a trick to represent himself as a marksman, and is consequently hired both by a Mafia organisation (The Society of the Blinking Buzzards) and as a bodyguard by the man the BB's are out to murder. The villains are routed in a showdown in a crazily booby-trapped house.

There are two possible explanations for Keaton's dislike. One is that though the characters he played varied considerably from film to film, Keaton had a firm conception of the moral basis of his comedy *persona*. 'Charlie's tramp was a bum with a bum's philo-sophy. Lovable as he was he would steal if he got the chance. My little fellow was a working-man and honest.' The hero of *The High Sign* is different from the rest in being positively larcenous. The first thing we see him do is steal a newspaper from a man passing by on a merry-go-round (the paper provides a good gag: he unfolds it . . . and unfolds it . . . and unfolds it until it is as big as a bedsheet). Subsequently he is seen replacing a policeman's pistol with a banana—which again provides subsequent gags: first when the policeman attempts to draw on the villain and finds himself pointing a piece of fruit; later when he has thrown down the banana skin. (Keaton was fond of quoting this instance of how a comedian loses by being too smart. He said that the surprise gag of *not* slipping on the banana skin and then making the Mafia 'high sign' fell entirely flat at the preview, so that he subsequently added another scene in which he *did* slip. The situation is no longer clear in extant copies.) Threatened by the shooting-gallery proprietor, who is also chief of the Buzzards, Buster rigs up an ingenious machine to fake his sharp-shooting prowess. When he steps on a hidden lever a system of wires and pulleys drops a bone in front of a bulldog which thereupon tugs at a cord which rings the target bell. Buster's fraud works admirably until a cat engages the dog's attention.

Apart from the hero's thefts and frauds, some of the gags have elements of the 'ridiculous' which Keaton's essentially realist and logical nature was eventually to reject. For instance he draws a hook with chalk on a wall and then hangs his coat on it; and the whole idea of the Blinking Buzzards is pretty absurd. And the rigged-up sectional house in which the finale takes place—a brilliantly choreographed mousetrap chase through pivoted panels and trapdoors in the floor—differs from other Keaton trick houses (in *The Scarecrow* and *The Electric House*, for instance) in that, though funny and clever, it is a massive stage prop imposed upon the character, rather than a natural expression of the hero's ingenuity.

One tiny piece of imagery deserves recalling. Buster sniffs a poisoned cup of tea; and his suspicions are confirmed by the super-imposition of a kicking mule on the close-up of the cup.

After *The High Sign* Keaton fulfilled his Metro feature contract. According to Keaton himself it was Mary Pickford and Douglas Fairbanks (who had himself played the role on Broadway and in his first film, *The Lamb*) who suggested Buster for the part of Bertie Van Alstyne in the film version of *The New Henrietta*. *The Saphead* (its up-dated 1920 title) was to be a big prestige production, running seven reels instead of the then customary five. The play dated back to 1887 when William Henry Crane (1845–1928), who plays the same role in *The Saphead*, created the character of Nicholas Van Alstyne, 'The Wolf of Wall Street', in Bronson Howard's *The Henrietta*. Written expressly for Crane and his then partner Stuart Robson, the play opened at the Union Square Theatre, New York. Crane continued to play the role for many years; and in December 1913 a sequel, *The New Henrietta*, was presented at the Knickerbocker Theatre. The film (directed by Herbert Blaché, though Winchell Smith, who had been responsible for the stage version, directed the players) seems to have been adapted from this later version. Today it appears as a pretty mild sort of comedy, about the fool of the family who, on his very first visit to the Stock Exchange, thwarts the villain and saves his family's fortunes. Keaton himself has comparatively little real comic business apart from a very charming scene in which—anxious to prove himself a true playboy in the eyes of his girl—he tries desperately and unsuccessfully to get himself arrested in a club raid; and some rather elegant comic tumbling in the stock-market scenes.

Nevertheless, in two respects *The Saphead* was probably crucial to his career. In the first place it definitely established him as a star in his own right. More important, although he never again played a character quite so idiotic as Bertie Van Alstyne—fate's fool and next door to an idiot—the experience in creating a sustained dramatic character (something he had not done since he played Little Lord Fauntleroy and Willie in *East Lynne*, apparently without much inner conviction, in 1906) almost certainly encouraged and helped him in the formulation of later Keaton characters: that variety of grave, contemplative, bravely resourceful souls who are the quiet and steady centre of the frenzy that is Keaton's world.

The first of these true Keaton heroes is the bridegroom of *One Week*. Apart from the joke title, and the quip that the film is only a third as passionate as *Three Weeks*, it has no relation to Elinor Glyn's then sensational novel. The real point of the title is that the film is given a very amusing time structure by introducing each sequence with a sequent page from a daily calendar. It opens with the happy couple leaving the church. (The girl, the first of a run of marvellous Keaton heroines, was Sybil Sealey.) On the steps Buster providently picks up a pair of boots that have been thrown

An early dramatic role as Little Lord Fauntleroy, 1906

along with the confetti. A note from Uncle Mike informs them that his present is a build-it-yourself house kit and a plot of land. Handy Hank, Buster's disappointed rival, has maliciously altered all the numbers on the boxes containing the house, so that when Buster begins to assemble it a very queer and crazed structure begins to rise up. By Tuesday the place is complete and Buster has a fight with a piano. Wednesday sees the catastrophe of laying the carpet. Thursday brings difficulties with a chimney-pot and bath.

'Friday the Thirteenth' sees the house-warming. As the guests are being shown the house, a storm comes on. The rain pours through the roof and the house starts to spin, faster and faster, hurling hosts and guests out of doors and windows. On Saturday, as the once-happy couple are sadly contemplating the ruins, a man comes along and tells them that they had built it on the wrong plot anyway. On Sunday they attempt to tow their home away behind the Model T. Breaking loose, it sticks on a railway track. In an effort to dislodge it, Buster nails the back seat of the car to the house; but when the car drives off, the chassis parts from the body. They hear a train coming, and cover their ears, but it passes safely by on a parallel track. As they are congratulating themselves, another train smashes straight through the house. Before they set off to walk away into the distance, Buster puts a 'For Sale' sign on the heap of debris—and leaves the instructions for the build-it-yourself house with it.

This beautifully composed little film, an accelerating merry-go-round of catastrophes, may be reckoned Keaton's first masterpiece. He is now clearly in his element, working out the sort of gags in which he delighted: an ingenious sequence in which he transfers from car to car in mid-traffic; an encounter with a disintegrating car; the most spectacular gag to this date with an express train. The whirlwind home, as well as providing some memorable Alice-in-Wonderland images, looks forward to *Steamboat Bill Jr.*; and the great gag of the house-side which falls down about the hero, framing him in the window-opening, first proposed in *Back Stage* and later to be perfected in *Steamboat Bill Jr.*, is tried out here on a larger scale.

Convict 13

One Week also reveals the somewhat melancholy cast to much
of Keaton's comedy; but nothing in any of the films is quite so
black as his next two-reeler, *Convict 13*. The fragmentary state in
which most copies of this film have survived only emphasises its
extreme strangeness. In the original form of the film, Buster is
playing golf when a ball hits him on the head. He has a nightmare
about being a prisoner who escapes from the scaffold with the help
of the governor's lovely daughter. Then he wakes up to find himself back on the golf course and being cared for by a beautiful girl
—the governor's daughter of the dream.

Such copies of the film as are presently available have mostly
lost the framework of reality, and contain only the gaol nightmare.
The visual quality of this is extraordinary, particularly when it is
found in original amber-tinted copies. The hard contrasts of the
black and white convict stripes have a physically disturbing effect
of dazzlement. The nightmare begins with Buster on the scaffold

The Scarecrow, with Joe Roberts and Sybil Sealey

about to be hanged in the presence of a demonstratively approving crowd of spectators, laughing, cheering and gobbling popcorn. The trap opens—and Buster bounces up and down on the end of the elastic which the girl has substituted for the hangman's rope. To the fury of his audience, Buster leaps to the ground and makes off.

Later, breaking rocks in the prison yard, he swings his hammer back too boldly and fells a guard, whose uniform he thereupon puts on. Meanwhile a giant convict has staged a one-man revolt and knocked out a whole procession of warders as they come at him through a door. He attacks Buster, who manages temporarily to worst him and is consequently promoted to assistant warder. A bigger mutiny follows, in the course of which the big convict makes off with the Governor's pretty daughter. But this riot, too, is quelled by Buster. The climax comes when he brings down the mutineers like skittles as he swings a ball and chain about his head.

The film, whose characteristic image is a courtyard piled with the unconscious bodies of prisoners or warders, has a disturbing quality of violence which never again appeared in Keaton's films, except, to a degree, in the brutal finale of *Battling Butler*.

The Scarecrow is altogether more genial and optimistic. Buster and his room-mate live in the first of the real mechanised houses ('All the rooms in this house,' says the title, 'are in one room'). The gramophone is convertible into a gas stove; a series of pulleys and strings produces things from the ice-box; a little train runs up and down the table conveying the rolls and butter. After the meal, all the eating equipment hides away; and the table-top is hung on a wall to reveal a text ('What is home without a mother') on the verso. The bath is turned on its side and becomes a sofa as the water empties through a trap into the duckpond. The bed tips up and turns into an organ.

Buster and his room-mate are bitter rivals for the farmer's daughter (Sybil Sealey again). She is a frolicsome little thing, forever prancing about in the accepted fashion of twenties heroines. ('She belonged to the Dancers Union,' says a caustic

Neighbors

title, 'and couldn't stop till the whistle blew.') Buster is involved in a chase with a dog which is foaming at the mouth from the effects of stealing a cream pie. The well-intentioned creature watches curiously as Buster is sucked into a harvest machine which strips him of all his clothes. He steals a scarecrow's outfit; and is then obliged to take the scarecrow's place. The end is excellent. When the girl finds Buster kneeling to do up his shoelace, she takes it for a proposal. They attempt to elope and leap upon a couple of horses standing by; but the one he has chosen turns out to be a dummy. He therefore vaults on to the back of hers; but misses. Pursued by the girl's father, they snatch a motor-bike. Tearing across the road, they sweep up a priest who happens to be passing. (Buster, suddenly finding the priest beside him, throws a momentary upward glance to inquire where he might have come from.) As the priest is pronouncing them man and wife, using a spare nut for a ring, the trio drive straight into a lake.

Keaton's growing concern with the visual qualities of his films is clear from the setting of *Neighbors*. The opening scene is a long shot of the valley between two high tenement buildings, the sun filtering down through chimney-pots and washing-lines. A fence between the two buildings exactly bisects the screen. Buster and his new leading lady Virginia Fox (who became Mrs Darryl Zanuck) are a Romeo and Juliet of the slums, their romance thwarted by the antagonisms of their respective families. The girl's father is played by Joe Roberts, an old vaudevillian who was to be Keaton's heavy until his death in 1923; Buster's father was Joe Keaton, who appears in the later scenes of the film with a broken arm, which is passed off in a gag subtitle: 'What happened to you?' 'I bought a Ford.'

The opening is an old vaudeville situation. Buster passes a note, 'I love you' through a knot-hole in the fence. It is intercepted by her father, who angrily pushes it back in time for Buster's mother to receive it, observed by her jealous husband. The note is pushed back again; and received by the girl's embarrassed father whose angry wife has by this time arrived on the scene. This provides the motive for a good deal of wild and ingenious chasing. At times the film develops into a vaudeville acrobatic comedy routine, with Buster and the two Joes and assorted policemen involved with clothes-lines, water-butts, loose fence-boards which batter behinds or heads, and Negroes. The ending, following an abortive marriage ceremony which opens with the bride sitting romantically upon a dustbin and ends abruptly with the descent of both the parson's and the bridegroom's trousers, has a nice surreal fantasy. A couple of acrobats, one on the other's shoulders, ply between the two high buildings so that Buster and the girl can leap from upper windows to stand on their shoulders. This four-storey column of people rushes along the road, splitting up to pass through three-tier scaffolding and rejoining again at the end. A clothes-line removes the middle acrobat; the bottom one falls through a man-hole; and finally Buster and the girl themselves fall through a stokehole. There they find the parson filling his stove. He marries them.

Keaton was now turning out shorts at the rate of one a month; but there was a two-month gap between the release of *Neighbors* and *The Haunted House*, which appeared in February 1921. *The Haunted House* and *My Wife's Relations*—which also, as it happened, followed a lengthy gap, four months this time, between releases—are unarguably the least successful of Keaton's own shorts. It is true that surviving copies of the earlier film are corrupt; but at times its disorganised frenzy looks more like an Arbuckle comedy. The situation is extravagantly and untypically absurd. Buster is a bank clerk who inexplicably arrives at work in a chauffeur-driven Rolls. The villainous bank-teller maintains a gang of men dressed as ghosts and phantoms to frighten people away from his house, which is in any event full of booby-traps. A visiting opera company doing *Faust* gets mixed up with the whole thing. The best sequence—and it is not very good—is some business with a pot of glue, much of which is lifted straight from *The Butcher Boy*. The climax of the scene is when Buster, his hands firmly glued in his pockets, is told by some hold-up men to put 'em up.

Keaton's own favourite among the shorts was *Hard Luck*, of

which no copy seems to have survived, though we can perceive a little of its quality from a marvellous still of Keaton sitting on the rear of a horse and facing aft, his eyes shaded against the sun, while a rather sportive-looking lady sits with her back to him, holding the reins. In the old two-reeler tradition the film seems to have fallen into two distinct halves. In the first Buster, weary of life, tries to commit suicide. He lies down on a railway track, but the points are changed and the train simply passes by on another line. He tries to hang himself, but the rope is too long. He drinks from a bottle marked poison; but since it is in fact Scotch, and he drinks deeply of it, he eventually shakes off his suicidal depression. The second half of the film takes place at a country club and relates Buster's difficulties as a fisherman, horseman and swimmer. Keaton recalled a fantastic gag with which he ended the film. The final scene takes place in the country club pool. After a terrific build-up on the high-dive board—flexing his muscles and ostentatiously testing the board and measuring distances—Buster does a great swan dive which misses the pool entirely. He crashes right through the adjoining cement walk, leaving a large hole. . . . The fadeout is succeeded by a title, 'Years later.' The pool is now seen empty and ruined; but the hole is still there; and Buster emerges from it, gone Chinese and followed by an Oriental wife and children. 'But that sort of gag I would never use in a full-length picture—because it could not happen in real life, it was an impossible gag.'

His next film, *The Goat*, was the first of a remarkable succession of five shorts, each made within a month and yet each one comparable in polish and accomplishment with his mature features. Keaton's usual co-director throughout the period of the two- and three-reelers was Eddie Cline. For *The Goat*, as for *The Blacksmith* the following year, Keaton worked instead with Mal St Clair, who had just left Sennett, differences of opinion between producer and director having come to a head, it seems, over a Ben Turpin film, *Bright Eyes*. The co-director was evidently simply one of the total creative team. Eddie Cline always gave full creative credit to Keaton; and Keaton recalled in relation to his co-

Eddie Cline (*left*); *The Goat* (*right*)

directors: 'Well, when we started making our own pictures we worked so different than a dramatic company and we knew what we had in our mind and a director would only help confuse you. And any time I'm out in front of the camera working if there was any technical flaws I only had to look at the cameraman and he'd tell me or one of the writers standing off the side or even the prop man sometimes says, "You can do that better." So, all right, let's try it again. So that's all there was to that.'

The Goat is distinguished (and it is impossible to say whether this was due in any way to the influence of St Clair) by its extreme complexity, the way in which gags are interwoven throughout the film. Near the start of the picture, for instance, there is a wonderful scene in which Buster (more of a simpleton here than usual) stares with rubber-neck curiosity through the bars of a police-station window. Wily Deadshot Dan, who is inside having his identity picture taken, bends down out of range of the camera lens and triggers the camera so that it is Buster, behind bars, who is photographed, after which Dan makes his escape. It is only in the second part of the film that this gag is taken up again, as the 'Wanted' posters identifying Buster as Dan begin to appear in the streets. At first bewildered, then terrified by this unexpected notoriety, Buster eventually turns it to his advantage by using

Dan's lethal reputation to frighten off a troublesome taxi-driver. There are other examples of this delayed gag development. Buster decoys a gang of policemen who are pursuing him into a pantech-nicon and shuts them in just as it moves off. Much later in the film, when we have forgotten the gag, the pantechnicon suddenly reappears, backs on to Buster, and the police all tumble out to resume the chase.

Between times he has gallantly knocked down a man whom he discovers insulting a pretty girl. Later, when he finds himself a wanted man, he supposes (as a one-shot flashback reveals) that he must have killed the man. The sudden appearance of the white and ghost-like figure of a man whom we have already seen in altercation with a plasterer, confirms his fears. Running off, Buster lands straight in the arms of a detective, who gives chase. Later, having eluded his pursuer, he meets the girl again. She takes him home to supper. When her father comes home, he turns out to be the same detective and the chase begins all over again. This structural intricacy, added to the tragic singleness of the theme— the totally innocent Buster becomes constantly more deeply embroiled with the police as the chase becomes more desperate— makes *The Goat* one of the most densely textured of all Keaton's films.

Gag inventions proliferate: Buster absent-mindedly standing behind two tailors' dummies under the impression that they are at the end of the free bread-line; leaping on to the spare tyre on the back of a car just as it is moving away only to find that the tyre is quite detached, a garage advertisement; hiding on the back of a clay model of an equestrian statue, which gradually sinks at the knees under his weight as it (and he) is publicly unveiled; luring the detective under a cart of logs, then collapsing the load on top of him, adding one extra small chip of wood for luck. For good measure there is one of the best train gags. Pursued by the police, Buster jumps on the back of a train; but as it moves away it slips its couplings, leaving Buster's part stationary and him looking foolish as he makes insolent gestures at the police. Suddenly recognising his predicament, he runs off after the train. He gets on the back of the train, runs through it, out on to the roof and slips the hind part of the train just as the police run through it. Iris out and in. From the far distance the train runs towards the camera. As it comes closer and into full close-up, we see that Buster is sitting on the cow-catcher. He walks off nonchalantly as the driver scratches his head on finding his train is mislaid.

After *The Goat*, Keaton's whole professional and private life underwent complete revolution. This was the last film he released through Metro. The Keaton Company bought the Lillian Way Studios and, still with Joseph Schenck as producer, began to release through First National as the Comique Film Company, and from mid 1922 as Buster Keaton Productions Inc. In late March or April 1921 Keaton broke his ankle on an escalator which was one of the elaborate props of his own devising for *The Electric House*. This accident resulted in a prolonged rest which seems, on the evidence of the brilliant run of work which followed it, to have been refreshing. It also necessitated the release of *The High Sign*, which Keaton had until now managed to suppress. During this period, too, Keaton contracted the marriage with Natalie Talmadge (sister-in-law of Joseph Schenck who had married the actress Norma Talmadge) which was to prove so unhappy and destructive to him, but which at the time seemed idyllic. The accident also persuaded Keaton to hire a regular special effects man; and the resourceful and inventive Fred Gabourie was to prove a valuable collaborator.

For his first film after resuming work, following the accident, Keaton had to devise something that would not require his usual kind of acrobatic business. The outcome was *The Playhouse*, one of his strangest and most wonderful shorts. Restricted as to his personal performance, Keaton set himself to solve a series of elaborate technical problems of multiple exposure. The film was also a direct reminiscence of vaudeville days: there are backstage scenes, a minstrel act, a precision dance act, an aquatic star (Annette Kellerman was a childhood idol), a performing ape (Keaton liked to reminisce about Peter the Great, a performing

Keaton's sister, Elgin Lessley, Virginia Fox, Keaton's mother, Keaton, Clyde Bruckman, Joe Mitchell, Harry Brand, *c.* 1922

animal who had been on the same bill as his family at the London Palace, in 1909). Buster himself performs the broom and knot-hole routine from stage days, and does the alarming dive through the backcloth which, in the family act, was known as his Original Aboriginal Dive. The mixture of memory and magic is potent: *The Playhouse* is the most dreamlike of all Keaton's films, deriving a surreal aura from its roots in his past and his subconscious.

Was the multiple exposure itself, one wonders, the effect of a childhood memory? Méliès' most remarkable trick film, *Le Mélomane*, had been released in America in 1903, when Buster was seven. It is more than likely that it would have been shown on some of the bills on which he played. Certainly the resemblance between Méliès' strange fantasy of the musical staff on which every note is a Méliès face mouthing and mugging in time to the music of 'God Save the King' has a striking echo in the rhythmical jiggings of the minstrel show in which every black face is the wide-eyed mask of Buster.

The film opens with Buster entering a theatre. Inside, every member of the orchestra is Buster. The audience—the swell and the belle in their box, the old dowager and her doddery husband, the Irish scrubwoman and her awful child—all have the face of Buster. The stagehand is Buster, the minstrels are all Buster, the soft-shoe act is a pair of Busters. . . .

The illusion is broken. Another, humbler Buster is asleep in his room. A big man roughly wakes him and begins to carry off the furniture and then the room itself. For the man and his assistants are not, as we for the first moment suppose, bailiffs, but stage-hands; and this is not a real bedroom but a stage set. And Buster himself is just another stagehand, caught napping and dreaming his Protean dreams.

Illusion succeeds illusion. Buster is bewildered by a pair of identical twins; and shattered when he sees them looking into mirrors so that there are four of them. The ultimate shock is to see his own reflection in a triple dressing-room mirror. He is in love with one of the girls, but he is never clear which one.

The range of Keaton's impersonations is extraordinary—not only the nine musicians or the seven orchestra members or the brat in the box who drops his lollipop on the elegant lady in the box below, who absently uses the half-sucked lollipop as a lorg-nette; but the monkey too—an astonishing characterisation, and (when he shins up the proscenium arch) one would have thought a perilous one for someone still nursing a broken ankle. It is a strange sensation to perceive among the memories a portent: the conductor whose music stubbornly cascades off its stand is in much the same plight as that older musician who accompanies Calvero in *Limelight*.

The technique for doing the brilliant multiple exposures in the minstrel and soft-shoe acts seems to have been devised by Keaton himself. He first had a special mask made to put over the lens, with nine shutters which could be opened one at a time. 'It was hardest for Elgin Lessley at the camera. He had to roll the film back eight times, then run it through again. He had to *hand-crank* at *exactly* the same speed *both* ways, *each* time. Try it sometime. If he were off the slightest fraction, no matter how carefully I timed my movements, the composite action could not have synchronised. But Elgin was outstanding among all the studios. He was a human metronome.'

'My synchronising was gotten by doing the routines to banjo music. Again, I got a human metronome. I memorised the routines very much as they lay out dance steps—each certain action at a certain beat in a certain measure of "Darktown Strutters' Ball." Metronome Lessley set the beat, metronome banjo man started tapping his foot, and Lessley started each time with ten feet of blank film as a leader, counting down, "Ten, nine, eight," and so on. At "zero"—we hadn't thought up "blast off" in those days—banjo went into chorus and I into routine. Simple.' (Quoted in Rudi Blesh, *Keaton*.)

The Boat can rank with the great feature-length comedies. It has the same kind of comic substance as *The Navigator*. Its hero is the quintessential Keaton, small, brave, indomitable, though catastrophe follows catastrophe with terrible inevitability, facing each misfortune with a great, still, sad stare and a resource which still remains equal to the next one.

The film begins with one of Keaton's favourite surprises. 'Eight bells and all's not well': we find the hero in a storm-tossed boat ... then discover that the boat is on dry land, and that it is rocked not by the sea but by one of Buster's small, unsmiling, bothersome sons. 'All finished and ready for launching.' Buster has built the boat in the cellar, but the exit door is too low. Undeterred, he removes a few bricks from the top of the openings and hitches the family Ford to tow it out. But he has not noticed that the boat is too wide as well as too high; and as it comes through the doorway it dislodges the foundations of the house, which collapses entirely. Buster, his wife and their sons regard the destruction with faces as inscrutable as that of Garbo at the end of *Queen Christina*. Buster inspects the debris. The lifeboat is wrecked, so he loads up the bath.

'There's more than one way to launch a boat.' Buster is towing the boat into position on the slipway when his attention is momentarily distracted (one of the children has got caught up somewhere). He drives straight over the dock edge. He gets out before the machine finally tips over: then peers curiously as it sinks in the harbour.

The boat, 'The Damfino,' is finally ready for launching. The skipper stands proudly on the deck. His wife tries to break a bottle of Cola on the stern, but the bottle stays intact while the stern is dented. Buster obligingly leans over the side and smashes the bottle with a hammer before preparing for one of the greatest single Keaton images. Proud and erect he stands on the prow of the boat as it goes slowly down the slipway—and down . . . and down . . . until the water comes up to Buster's neck and his head suddenly swivels round in helpless bewilderment.

But 'You can't keep a good boat down.' 'The Damfino' is at last seaworthy and ready for its odyssey of disaster. Buster puts the funnel down on top of one of the children, then, recognising the cries from within, picks it up, neatly ejecting the child into the water. Then he has to go in after the child. He forgets to untie the boat and carries off the mooring-post together with a fisherman who happens to be sitting on top of it. He is crowned by a funnel, for he has fixed up all the deck gear like a ship in a bottle so that it can all be collapsed in order to go under low bridges; and has another ducking. He casts the anchor; which promptly floats to the surface. 'Ten seconds later . . .' says a title mad enough for *L'Age d'Or.*

After lunch—a touching family affair with Buster and the boys in complicity not to let on to mother that her pancakes are too tough to eat—the troubles start again. Buster nails a picture to the cabin wall, and springs a leak. One of the pancakes comes in handy to patch it. The boat is practically capsized by a sporty passing motor launch. They all go to bed (the children in night-shirts and their little Buster hats), but Buster has difficulties with his bunk. Then he is washed out of bed by a sudden assault of water through the porthole.

A storm rises. Buster gamely tackles it with, successively, a candle, an umbrella and a telescope; but they are all washed overboard; and he follows them. He radios the coastguards for help; but when, in reply to their request for identification, he replies 'Damfino,' they curtly reply: 'Neither do I,' and shut down on him.

The boat is turned over and over. The leak bursts open again, and despite Buster's ingenious efforts to drain the water out of new holes which he bores in the floor, it sinks. The family are set adrift in the bath, leaving Buster to go down gallantly with his ship. When his little hat floats by, they bow their heads . . . until Buster rises up underneath the hat, which he is actually still wearing. The family are reunited in the bath. One of the children asks for a drink of water, and Buster obligingly gets it out of the bath tap. While the parents are trying to summon help, the smaller child playfully pulls the plug out of the bath and throws it away.

As they sink, Buster encloses them in an embrace, and closes his eyes. A moment later he opens them again as the bath touches bottom. Hand in hand the little family get out of the bath and walk off into the darkness. They turn for a moment. 'Where are we?' Buster mouths, 'Damfino' . . . and they vanish into the night.

No Keaton film previous to *The Boat* was quite so sustained in its melancholy; or provided such continuous laughter.

The Boat had somewhat taxed the ingenuity of Keaton's new special effects man. Keaton recalled to Rudi Blesh that Gabourie had made two boats, one to float and one to sink, but that they persistently performed each other's functions.

The astonishing thing about the whole series of nineteen shorts released between September 1920 and March 1923 is their variety. Keaton never repeats a gag or a story structure. Every film seems to be an experiment towards the mature work of the features. *The Paleface*, for instance, anticipates *The General* in its use of large masses of people against natural backgrounds; and *Our Hospitality* and *The Navigator* in the way that the comedy is predicated by a serious dramatic situation. The film opens with white oil prospectors cheating Indians out of their lands. The Indians resolve: 'Kill the first white man who comes through the gate'; and of course that white man is a solemn little figure in a flat hat, collecting butterflies.

The first part of the film is concerned with Buster's efforts to frustrate the Indians' wish to burn him. After he has made himself an asbestos suit and cheerfully smoked a cigarette at the pyre, the Indians all fall down and worship him. In the role of their leader he argues their cause with the oil traders. Subsequently, however, after one of the traders forces him at gunpoint to change clothes with him, Buster has again to flee from his own tribe. All is explained finally, and he returns to marry the chief's daughter. They fall into a passionate clinch. Title: 'Two years later.' They are discovered still in the same clinch which they resume after a brief pause for breath.

Up to *The Goat* Keaton shorts had been composed of eight gags. The best parts of *The Playhouse* depended upon technical virtuosity. *The Boat* was very much a prop film. The most important parts of *The Paleface*, however, are those which depend upon the agility and daring which was to play so large a part in the great features. Keaton does a hair-raising leap into a tree. He slides down a perilous forty-five-degree gravel slope. His most astonishing feat is to cross a ravine by a bridge which consists of staves slung across two wires. But only a few of the staves remain and he must crawl across, taking staves from behind him and planting them ahead. Even this feat is capped. He is fleeing from Indians. Arriving at the opposite side of the bridge he finds a different hostile tribe waiting for him. He therefore plunges into the ravine below. Already he had understood the special potency of these perilous gags—performed as easily as breathing, it seemed, and filmed without fakery, in all-revealing, long-take long-shots as frank in their gaze as Keaton himself.

The astonishing run of successes reached its climax and its end in *Cops*. The working-out of this film has the inevitability of tragedy; and the melancholy underlying *The Goat* and *The Boat* is here more than ever pronounced. Buster's 'working man, and honest' is thrust by fate and in perfect, ignorant innocence, into the role of a criminal; and in this role he is forced into opposition with the entire New York police force. The ending is very peculiar, and much nearer tragedy than farce.

The film opens with a Keaton surprise. We see him disconsolate behind bars. The camera moves back to take in a larger view, and we see that he is in fact gazing through the girl friend's garden gate. A series of confusions with a taxi and an aggressive fat policeman leave him the surprised possessor of the policeman's wallet (and already, in consequence, a criminal). He falls victim to a con-man who, on the pretext that his wife and children are starving, sells the soft-hearted Buster the contents of someone else's home. The true owner is a policeman who is actually moving house, so that when Buster starts to load his goods into a horse-cart he has just bought, the man is not surprised, taking him for the removal man. Buster himself is a little taken aback when the stranger helps him load. His trip through the town, negotiating busy urban traffic with a horse which is deaf as well as unwilling, proves to be the usual Keaton confrontation of disaster and re-sourcefulness.

All at once he finds himself at the head of the annual New York police parade. He is only momentarily surprised by the cheering which he graciously acknowledges as if it were meant for him. Suddenly (a direct reference to the 1919 Wall Street outrage and all the other post-war bomb scares) anarchists on the roof of a building throw down a bomb, which lands on the seat beside him. Absently he lights a cigarette from its burning fuse, and throws the thing over the side. It explodes, wrecking the parade and panicking the crowd. The whole of the police force is now in pursuit of Buster: a wild chase sequence ends with him using a ladder to catapult himself to safety over the heads of the police who have surrounded him.

The concluding sequence begins with a shot of an empty street —a strange perspective view like a Palladian stage setting, seen through a great archway. Keaton comes into view round the corner; and a moment later, after him, a huge army of policemen. They all move forward and disappear out of the bottom of the frame, to reappear a moment later and retrace their steps, the police still in pursuit of the little lone figure. They follow him into a doorway. The camera draws back: it is the police station. The doors close behind them. A moment or two later a figure in police uniform stealthily comes out of the door, shutting it and locking it behind him. It is, of course, Buster. The girl—the one from the garden of the beginning of the film whom we subsequently saw sitting beside the mayor in the reviewing stand—passes by. She cuts him. He unlocks the door and goes back into the police station. The 'End' title is written on a gravestone, on which is perched Buster's flat hat.

Following on the high comedy of the cart-ride through the town—Buster striding the back of the piled-up cart like the captain on the bridge of a ship; or rigging up a telephone to communicate with the deaf horse; or fixing up a system of mechanical hand signals (which naturally punch a policeman) after his protruding hand has been bitten by a passing dog—the strange and surrealist melancholy of the end is as mysterious as it is haunting.

It is hardly surprising that Keaton could not sustain the level of the miraculous period between *The Goat* and *Cops*; and none of the six films he made between *Cops* and his last (and now lost) two-reeler, *The Love Nest*, equals the quality of his best work. It may be, too, that his personal life was for the first time providing strains and distractions. In the early part of 1922 his wife was expecting her first child, and Keaton was moving house, forced, apparently against his temperament, to live up to the regal image of a twenties movie star. Between February and June there was no Keaton release (although *The Playhouse*, *The Boat*, *The Paleface* and *Cops* had all appeared within a period of four months); and then came *My Wife's Relations*, perhaps the least distinguished of all Keaton's silent films. It begins quite nicely. A big Irishwoman catches Buster accidentally breaking a window, and marches him off to a judge who, not speaking English, marries them by mistake. The woman carries home her unexpected prize to her awful family, who treat him with the utmost disrespect until they think he is to inherit a fortune. They then move into a ritzy apartment and take up lives of leisure until the true state of affairs emerges and Buster makes a getaway on a train bound for Reno.

It is an untidy and intermittent affair, the best scenes being a fight with a bed; and a family meal at which Buster, as a result of his politeness, is always left behind until he has the bright idea of changing the calendar to Friday's date, whereupon the greedy but devout Irish put back their steaks. The uninhibited clouts which Buster lays on his virago bedmate, under cover of being asleep, are also very funny; and her appearance in society with her bird's nest of hair unaccountably crowned with an apple for decoration, is not bad.

In *The Blacksmith* Keaton again had Mal St Clair as his co-director; but the results are not in any respect equal to *The Goat*. As a series of gags arising not out of a developing story situation but exploiting the comic possibilities of a particular setting, the film harks back to the Arbuckle films (and there are obvious resemblances to *The Garage*). Keaton is the blacksmith's assistant. He fries eggs on the forge. There is a good deal of business with a huge hanging magnet which attracts any loose bits of metal, including the blacksmith's hammer and the sheriff's badge. Buster does a very charming routine of fitting out a horse with new shoes in the manner of a human shoe shop, selecting different models from boxes stacked around the wall, and, like a polite salesman, consulting the horse's taste. He fits up a motor-car springing system under the saddle of a sore lady rider. He manages systematically to destroy two cars—an old crock and a brand-new white Rolls—in a single operation. Later he admitted that the Rolls was a mistake. Like W. C. Fields, he discovered from the reception of his films, 'You usually can't get a laugh out of damaging anything valuable. When you kick a silk hat, it must be dilapidated; when you wreck a car, bang it up a little before you bring it on the scene' (W. C. Fields, writing in 1924).

The film only acquires the authentic Keaton flavour towards the end. Buster saves a pretty girl when her horse bolts. She presses money on him. Insulted, he rejects it angrily and nobly, hurling the coins to the floor into some straw. But he is nothing if not practical. When the girl has gone he scrabbles in the straw and retrieves the money. The final scenes find him more on home ground, in a railway marshalling yard, foiling his pursuers (the blacksmith and the owner of the Rolls) with a water-feed. The actual finish is quaint. Buster and the girl make off in a train. Next we see a distant shot of the train crossing the bridge. Suddenly, it is derailed and falls off . . . and we realise that it is a toy train, with which Buster, domestic in his dressing-gown and smoking a pipe, is playing, while the girl, now his wife and holding a baby, looks on.

The succeeding four films, it must be acknowledged, are as polished as any of Keaton's work; but to a certain extent assurance and a degree of satisfaction with methods already exploited take the place of inspiration and invention. This may be a personal and disputable view; but it seems likely that Keaton had by this time outgrown the short-film form and was ready and waiting for the challenge of feature construction. (At the outset, before he began production in his own studio, he suggested to Schenck that he make only features in the future: 'But he wouldn't agree. Schenck insisted I return to the two-reel field. I couldn't convince him that comedy features were the coming thing. If I'd won that argument it could have made a big difference in my career. Neither Chaplin nor Lloyd were making features at that time, and I would have had a head start on both of them.')

The Electric House, it is true, had the ideal Keaton formula. (The material shot before the accident was all abandoned and the film was entirely reshot in a new set created by Gabourie, though using the original story.) Buster is given the wrong diploma by his correspondence college, and is thus qualified as an electrical engineer. He is commissioned to equip an all-electric house; and demonstrates to its happy owners all its escalators, dinner-table railways, washing-up machines and automated swimming-pool. When a prospective purchaser (Big Joe Roberts) comes to inspect it, the house is sabotaged by Buster's nefarious rival. The washing-up machine breaks all the crockery; the escalators hurl unsuspecting

Daydreams

ascenders into the swimming-pool; the service railway delivers cats and kittens instead of dinner. Finally the swimming-pool which empties and fills in thirty seconds flat (a pleasant use of accelerated motion, a device otherwise rare in Keaton films) empties, carrying Keaton down the plug-hole and out through the Los Angeles sewer into the sea.

From vaudeville days Keaton had enjoyed parody; and in *The Frozen North* he did a cod on a W. S. Hart Western. The satire came sufficiently near its mark—particularly in its teasing of Hart's tendency to cry, in a manly way, in emotional crises—for the great Western idol to take offence. The superimposition of the refinements of urban living upon the rugged West—the subway station from which the hero first emerges; the taxi-sledge which suddenly pulls up in the midst of the white wilderness—and such jokes as Keaton's raggy dog team which goes all to pieces at the sight of a rabbit, are entertaining. But the device of making the central character a take-off of another character simply does not work. The hero has no sort of consistency, either as a Keaton character or as a sustained parody figure. There are other memorable jokes, such as the outraged husband's entrance into a house where a man and a woman are in each other's arms. He shoots them; then realises that he does not know either of them: he has come to the wrong house. But *The Frozen North* is best regarded as a lark, Keaton's celebration of a temporary freedom from the domestic cares that were beginning to close in on him. (It was shot away from the studios, near Lake Tahoe in the High Sierras, where later he was to make *Our Hospitality* and the underwater scenes of *The Navigator*.)

It is not easy to assess *Daydreams*, since the copies that are available seem to be very incomplete. This is perhaps Keaton's most elaborate attempt to contrast and interweave dream and reality in the way that he had done or was to do in *Convict 13*, *The Playhouse*, *The Love Nest* and *Sherlock Junior*. The framing devices are the letters which Buster writes to his girl, whom he has left in order to prove himself worthy of her. He writes that he is 'cleaning up in Wall Street.' She dreams of an elegant wizard of the ticker-tape; the reality is a street-cleaner. He writes that he is an actor. She imagines a Hamlet Buster; the fact is that he is an extra having terrible trouble with his spear and finally getting thrown out of the theatre. The idea is, generally speaking, more attractive than the execution; and the return to the girl and the relationship between them is not managed with Keaton's usual clear grasp of character. The finale, however, is memorable. Running—for some reason—from the police, Buster leaps from the jetty on to a ferryboat—only to find that it is not as he had thought going out, but coming in. He therefore escapes from a window and on to the great paddle-wheel which begins to move round and round. To keep from going under the water, he must keep going round it like a mouse in a treadmill, endlessly.

Keaton never commented on *The Balloonatic* in the many interviews of his later years; but it is not likely that it would be among his favourites. It has too much of the quality which he

The Balloonatic

called 'ridiculous' to appeal to his logical nature. The film is really a discontinuous series of gags. The opening is a Keaton surprise. We find him in a darkened room, in which ghosts and devils and skeletons appear. The explanation only comes when he falls through a trapdoor and is ejected from a chute in front of a fairground side-show, the Haunted House. He watches curiously as a fat girl goes into the show; then a moment later she, too, comes down the chute, to land bang on top of Buster. Ruefully he watches her go back for another go, and sets off in the opposite direction. He gallantly lays down his jacket for a beautiful girl waiting at a muddy kerbside; but it is squashed in the dirt by the car for which she has been waiting. He follows another pretty girl into the Tunnel of Love and comes out with his hat bashed down about his eyes. Inquisitively he climbs on to a balloon which is being prepared for ascent. It breaks loose, and goes up with Buster on top of it. We see him later quite adjusted to his situation and

The Love Nest

hanging out his laundry to dry on the rigging. He hangs out some clay pigeons, and tries a little target practice; but manages to puncture the balloon.

He comes down in wild country where a nature girl (the statuesque and very funny Phyllis Haver) has pitched her camp. In the course of Buster's various experiments in boating (his eminently collapsible canoe is called the 'Minnie Tee Hee'), fishing, hunting and grilling his fish on a tennis racket, they get acquainted and strike up a warm enmity. But when Buster saves Phyllis from a cow and then accidentally shoots a bear, love blooms. We see them sailing off in their canoe. In long-shot we see them approaching a fall over an immense cliff. But the canoe sails straight on into the sky. It seems a perfect image of the invulnerability of lovers, until we see that the balloon has reappeared to hook itself on to the canoe and snatch the lovers from the brink.

Unhappily Keaton's last two-reeler, *The Love Nest*, is lost. All we have of it is the beautiful still almost invariably attributed to *The Navigator* which shows Buster attached by his feet to the rigging of a ship, sticking out over the ocean at an impossible forty-five-degree angle to the vertical, in a sailor suit and flat cap and scanning the high seas through a pair of binoculars. The film, so far as we can judge it, could almost have been a sketch for *The Navigator*, except that at the end of the picture his daring adventures on the high seas and under them in a submarine turn out to have been only a dream. He wakes up to find himself in his little motor boat, still safely moored at the quayside.

Now Schenck felt it was time to move into feature production. Two-reelers no longer took a worthwhile share of the rentals; and on the other hand, severely taxed resources of comedy material. From March 1923 the Keaton Studios changed their production policy. Henceforth instead of eight shorts each year the studios were to make two features. Keaton's salary was raised to $2,000 a week (later further increased by $500) while he maintained his 25-per-cent interest on the net profits.

5: *The Three Ages*

The first of the independent feature-length comedies was *The Three Ages*, made in the early summer of 1923 and released in August. The basic joke of the film is one which was then enjoying a vogue in newspaper cartoons and comic literature: an anachronistic view of historical periods—past times viewed as contemporary life in period disguise. *The Three Ages* illustrates the unchanging troubles and triumphs of love as they might have appeared in the Stone Age, in classical Rome and as they are in 1923. The form of the film, which followed its stories through parallel episodes, had a double advantage. On the one hand the parody of *Intolerance* would be readily recognised and appreciated. On the other it minimised Keaton's problems in tackling for the first time the construction of a six-reel film. *The Three Ages* is virtually three two-reelers, ingeniously interwoven. It even seems possible that Keaton may have contemplated a subsequent re-editing of the picture into its component shorts, if his feature career had proved less promising than in fact it turned out.

The staging of the film was ambitious (was the big arena set, one wonders, built for the film or was it left over from some earlier spectacle?), but not in any way as stylish as his next film *Our Hospitality*, or *The General*. In the later films the period settings and costumes, though gently caricatured, are essentially realistic and much of the comic effect comes from playing gags against the picturesque elegance of period accessories. Here the sets and

The Three Ages: Roman (*left*) and Modern (*right*)

costumes—Stone-Age Buster's fuzzy wig and enormous fur bootees for instance—are in themselves jokes.

Remarkably, composing his stories in exact parallel and finding period equivalents for the same sets of incidents, Keaton avoids any monotony or repetition. The first group of sequences for instance, introduces us to the principal characters: Beauty, her parents, the Adventurer (Wallace Beery) and the Faithful Worshipper at Beauty's Shrine (Buster). Beauty's parents supervise her choice of mate; the Faithful Worshipper consults oracles ('A troubled heart ever yearns to know the future' says the title, nicely catching the tones of a Griffith title-writer). In the Stone Age sequence the rival suitors arrive to court the girl on the backs of mastodon and dinosaur; the parents assess them by clubbing them energetically about various parts of the body (Buster having watched Beery calmly undergoing the test, braces himself, and falls spectacularly at the first gentle tap on the head); the sooth-

sayer is a marvellously crazy-looking old lady whose 'wee-gee' is a tortoise crawling about on a slab of rock and which bites Buster's finger.

In the Roman sequence the transport joke lies in the contrast between Beery's natty Ben-Hur chariot and Buster's soap-box conveyance, drawn by a dreadful quartet of ill-matched and seedy animals (the sweet white mare from *Cops* in harness with a mule, a donkey and something indescribable). The Roman soothsayer is an old fellow in a wizard's hat who operates by throwing dice (with Roman numerals of course). Some passing Negro litter-bearers jettison their protesting fare and join in the game. In the modern sequence ('The age of speed, need and greed') the gag is a race between Buster's Model T and Beery's custom-built special. They are neck and neck when Buster hits a slight bump in the road and his car collapses into a heap of wreckage. The modern parents judge the suitors by their bank-books; the modern Buster

The Three Ages →

The Three Ages, with Blanche Payson

does 'she loves me, she loves me not' with a flower, but the dramatic gesture with which he plucks the last, tragic petal is cut short by a wasp lurking at the centre.

The other episodes are varied with the same inventiveness. The second 'movement' shows the three Buster-heroes endeavouring to arouse jealousy in their prospective mates. Stone-Age Buster flirts with a reclining woman, but when he tries to emulate Beery's flirtatious way of dragging girls off by their hair, the lady stands up and shows herself to be a clear eighteen inches taller than himself. (The actress was a six-foot-three ex-policewoman, called Blanche Payson.) Roman Buster picks on a judo expert. The modern sequence is more elaborate (skilfully, the emphasis given to the individual stories is varied from episode to episode). Buster follows Beery and the girl into a restaurant. Unknown to him a previous diner has emptied a flask of bootleg gin into the water-carafe on Buster's table. A few swigs make Buster reckless and he

The Three Ages, with Margaret Leahy

makes up to the girl at a neighbouring table, to arouse the heroine's jealousy. Before leaving the restaurant, Beery sends a compromising note purporting to come from Buster to the strange girl, whose escort throws Buster out of the dining-room. Buster is last seen purposefully making his way out of the restaurant on wobbly knees, walking into a cab and straight out of the off-side door, and insistently pressing a note on the astonished cabby before vanishing into the night.

The third movement of the film brings the rival lovers into direct contest. Stone-Age Buster cheats in a club duel and is sent into the wilderness tied to the tail of a mammoth (a melancholy elephant, heavily disguised). This time the Roman episode is most elaborate. Although this was three years before the film version, General Wallace's *Ben Hur* and the stage success adapted from it had passed into legend. Keaton as a child in vaudeville must have played on the same bill as the 1907 Kalem film piracy, with its five-chariot race. In *The Three Ages* Keaton stages a chariot race; but to enhance its lunacy he plays it in a heavy snow-storm. Challenged by Beery he looks sadly at his shaggy chariot team, seeing them in imagination as four cardboard cut-outs, labelled 'Spark Plug.' Then he has another, inspirational, vision. In his imagination the chariot's wheels turn to sledge-runners.

When the contestants enter the snow-covered arena, Buster's sledge chariot is drawn by four huskies. He overcomes every set-back. When Beery's villainous slave diverts the dogs with a mangy cat, Buster ties the animal on a spear and uses it as a carrot to urge them on. When the dogs suddenly sit down, Buster solicitously inspects the off-side animal's paws; finding it defective, he swaps it for a spare in the box at the back of his chariot. He wins the race; but the sequence ends with Beery and his slave dropping him down a trapdoor to share a cell with a lion.

Here the modern section is weakest: a ball-game which allows Buster some virtuoso falls, with Beery engineering his arrest by slipping a flask of bootleg liquor into his pocket and then informing on him to a prohibition agent.

The film has thus arrived at a point where all its three heroes are in cliff-hanging situations. Keaton's sense of dramatic structure was already finely developed. Despite the difficulty of sustaining not one but three comic-dramatic climaxes, the fourth section of the film unerringly builds up its pace and intensity. Stone-Age Buster, returning from his trip on the mammoth's tail, snatches up the girl just as she is about to be married to Beery. The climax of a battle of dexterous rock-hurling (Clyde Bruckman recalled that Keaton made an altogether exceptional number of seventy-six takes to get a scene in which, in a single shot, a rock is hurled at him and then batted accurately back to brain the man who threw it) has Buster catapulted from a bent tree to hit Beery feet-first in the chest and rescue the girl. The fade-out shows a triumphant Buster dragging off his ecstatic bride by her hair.

The last two sequences of the film are the first fully developed instance of the extended 'trajectory' gags with which Keaton climaxed most of his subsequent features, and which in skill and rhythm of performance, timing and editing, no other comedian ever equalled. Roman Buster, after an engaging passage with the lion ('He vaguely remembered that somewhere—sometime—somehow—somebody made friends with a lion by doing something to its paws'), escapes from his cell to learn that the girl is in Beery's clutches. In a continuous movement he snatches a shield from an astonished soldier, leaps between the legs of two others converging on him, so that they collide, runs up a flight of steps, snatches a spear from a sentry, leaps on the back of a horse, pole-vaults from a standing position on the horse's back through an upper window. Finding the girl with Beery he pushes two pillars apart, Samson fashion, and brings the ceiling crashing down. He turns in momentary self-congratulation, only to be crowned by a belated falling stone. Snatching the girl, he slides down the spear which he has left leaning against the window. The fade-out is anti-climactic. He and the girl leap into a waiting litter which is borne off. The bottom falls out, leaving the couple on the ground in a compromising embrace.

The denouement of the modern story has to cap this. Buster, having discovered that Beery is a wanted criminal, escapes from the police station. Pursued, he runs up a fire-escape to the top of a high building. The subsequent trajectory, of great speed and brilliant execution, is accomplished in seven shots:

1. L.S. Parapets of two adjacent six-storey buildings; streets and traffic visible in the chasm below them. Buster, using fire-escape apparatus as springboard, leaps from left parapet to right, catches at opposite ledge but falls . . .
2. L.S. Profile of right-hand buildings with window awnings at each level. Buster falls straight through canvas of upper two awnings, but catches hold of third.
3. M.S. Awning. Buster climbs through awning frame and catches hold of drain-pipe, which comes loose.
4. L.S. Side of building, lower section. Buster clings to top of drain-pipe as a long section of it comes loose and circles down, pivoting about its lower end and projecting him into a window two storeys lower down.

5. M.S. Interior fire-house dormitory. Slide pole going down through aperture in centre of floor. Buster shoots through window at left, and slides down the pole.
6. M.S. Interior fire-house. Pole coming down from ceiling aperture. Fire-engine moving out of doors at left of screen. Buster slides down pole and leaps on back of fire-engine just as it moves out.
7. The fire. It is at the police-station from which Buster has just escaped. The fire-engine arrives, and Buster loyally leaps off with the firemen, snatching up a hatchet to help. Suddenly recognising where he is, he shyly replaces the hatchet on the engine and walks off.

Keaton was always conscientious about rounding off his stories. Buster grabs the girl from the church, carries her off in a taxi and reveals Beery's true villainy. They alight at the door of the girl's home. Buster is about to get back into the cab when the girl beckons him. At first he is shy and uncomprehending. Then she kisses him. He throws his hat in the air in a veritable explosion of ecstasy: 'Back to the church!' He grabs her and pulls her back into the cab. A funny little coda to the film shows the caveman Buster with his wife and eleven fur-clad infants. The Roman couple are followed by five graceful children in togas. The modern pair come out of their suburban villa followed by . . . a pekinese.

While he may have skirted problems of construction and sustained characterisation, in other respects Keaton exercised his virtuosity to the full. He was required to devise no less than thirteen effective fade-outs, and a high concentration of gags. It is hardly surprising if a few gags show a degree of contrivance. At the best of times the anachronistic joke is liable to date; and some of the gags here—Stone-Age golf; the helmet strap with which Roman Buster locks his chariot wheels—have faded somewhat while other allusions may have altogether lost their point; though the charm of the spare-wheel dog remains entire. Other jokes about contemporary manners still seem pointed. Tipsy, Buster watches in amazement as a girl in the restaurant makes up her face. Not to be outdone, he borrows her vanity case, gets a razor, shaving-soap and brush out of his pocket, and proceeds to shave in the table water.

But despite the charm of some of the jokes, the virtuosity of the balletic gag trajectories of the fourth reel, *The Three Ages* seems to belong to the period of the shorts, just as *The Boat* is the prototype of the great features. The leap from *The Three Ages* to the masterpiece *Our Hospitality* is one of the most startling revolutions in Keaton's career.

6: *Our Hospitality*

The Keaton company went on location for *Our Hospitality* almost as soon as *The Three Ages* was finished; and it was released in November 1923, only four months afterwards. The story, from an idea by Jean Havez, was based on the distinctly unhumorous incident of the Hatfield-McCoy feud. (Keaton called his feuding families Canfield and McKay.) The location scenes were shot in the beautiful country of the Truckee River and Lake Tahoe, between California and Nevada, and 300 miles due north of Los Angeles. The film was something of a family affair: Natalie Talmadge Keaton plays the heroine; Joe Keaton has a substantial role as the driver of the 'Rocket,' and his famous and lethal high kick is preserved for posterity in a scene where he kicks off the high hat of a doddering old train guard. The Keaton's fifteen-month-old son is seen in the prologue. Joe Roberts, a friend from vaudeville days and Keaton's heavy since *One Week*, was ailing during shooting and was to die a few weeks after completing his role as the father of the Canfield family.

Our Hospitality—with *The General* one of Keaton's most perfect films—is built with the dramatic integrity of a high adventure story. The prologue, indeed, is a completely serious affair of murder and revenge. Keaton, who constantly reiterated his conviction that comedy must never be 'too ridiculous' was evidently adopting a similar approach to Billy Wilder, who explained his reason for starting *Some Like It Hot* (1959) with a realistic staging of the St Valentine's Day Massacre as the need to give a sufficient weight of motive to the comic action. Establishing in this way the seriousness of the Canfield-McKay feud, Keaton provides a motive force for the entire plot.

One dark and stormy night a woman and her baby sit trembling in a hut. Outside, a flash of lightning momentarily reveals two figures. Two guns blaze (and the scene is so vividly shot that we seem to hear them, too). A second flash of lightning reveals the two men lying dead. In the Canfield home the head of the clan resolves: 'Now the feud must go on and on. . . .' The next day the widow McKay leaves her little hut to take her baby boy to New York.

Twenty years later the baby Willie McKay is a New York dandy. Summoned to take possession of his family estate, he pictures to himself a beautiful white colonial mansion. His aunt tells him the story of the Canfield-McKay feud.

The next reels of the film relate the rigours of train travel in pioneer railroad days. (Keaton was scrupulous: the action is set in 1831, two years after the first locomotives were imported from England.) With a capricious driver and a dotard guard with a post-horn, the train and its passengers suffer varied calamities. Country-folk along the route stop and stare; the cows scatter; an old man hurls stones and gratefully retrieves the firewood flung back at him in retaliation. The track corrugates as it passes over a series of fallen logs, and is temporarily bent to go around a donkey who cannot be politely persuaded to move out of the way. Varying a favourite Keaton chase joke, the train becomes unhooked, diverges from the locomotive on a twin track and rejoins the main track ahead of the engine, to the driver's bewilderment.

On the journey, Willie has befriended a girl. Arriving in town she runs to meet her family: the Canfields. Willie inquires the way to his paternal home from a stranger who is standing by—a Canfield again. The next section of the film shows Willie eluding pursuit by the two Canfield sons, in entire innocence that they are after him. One of the brothers comes after him with a gun, which jams as he attempts to fire it. Willie, noticing his plight, courteously

83

Our Hospitality: Leonard Chapman, Craig Ward, Joe Roberts, Monty Collins, Natalie Talmadge and Keaton →

Our Hospitality: Natalie Talmadge (*above*)

puts it right, incidentally almost shooting off his own foot. When the brothers arrive at a piece of river where Willie is fishing, he is providentially, if uncomfortably concealed by a sudden waterfall produced by the bursting of a dam.

Evening: Willie has innocently accepted the Canfield girl's invitation to dinner. Inside the house he overhears the brothers resolve to kill him, and their father's injunction that the laws of Southern hospitality forbid that he should be harmed while a guest under their roof. Supper is understandably nervy; and Willie is visibly alarmed by the sharpening of the carving knife. Afterwards he temporises to avoid leaving the house and exposing himself to the perils of the feud. He tries, for instance, to mislay his hat, but is foiled by his faithful dog (which has followed him from New York, trotting easily along between the back wheels of the train) who persistently retrieves it. Finally he uses the excuse of a rainstorm to extend his visit overnight.

Our Hospitality

Next morning his problem remains: to leave the house and run the watchful guard of the Canfield family. He makes a break disguised as a female servant; but a tucked-up skirt exposes his trousers at the back and the chase is on. One of the Canfield boys corners him on a cliff-face; and some acrobatics on the two ends of a rope running over a jut of rock end with the two antagonists in the river. At this moment the train re-enters the plot. As it chances to pass by on the river bank, Willie leaps on to the engine. As he bestrides engine and tender, they become uncoupled. He is left on the tender which leaps the rail to shoot into the water, and becomes an improvised boat for him. Shooting the rapids, Willie is swept overboard. The rope is still tied around his middle and entangles with a floating log.

Willie is swept downstream, still tied to the log which catches on some rocks at the edge of a waterfall of Niagara dimensions and ferocity. He scrambles on to a rocky ledge, still inextricably tangled with his rope and log. Meanwhile the girl has put off in a boat intending to rescue him, but is herself capsized. She is swept helplessly towards the fall. Willie sees her plight, and at the very moment when she goes over the falls, swings a half-circle on the end of his rope to seize her and swing her to safety on a lower ledge. At the very moment that his log comes loose and crashes over the falls, Willie manages to extricate himself. Joining the girl on her ledge, the two of them go off with the parson who has arrived at the riverside.

Later the Canfields return home, disappointed but determined to resume their murderous search the next day. Astonished to find their quarry in the girl's room, they are still more amazed to find that the parson has just married her and Willie. Canfield decides that it is time to end the feud.

The distinction of *Our Hospitality* is the complete dramatic logic with which it moves from the Prologue to the final reconciliation of the feuding families. It is constructed not as a progression of gags but as an integral adventure story in which the narrative incidents all have a comic slant. The only section of the film which at first sight appears disproportionate to the narrative development, a comic indulgence, is the extended train sequence; but even this has a number of strictly narrative functions: (1) It provides neutral ground on which to introduce Willie to the girl, to involve them without necessarily identifying themselves to each other as members of the feuding families. (2) It introduces the dog, which later has a small role in the scene where Willie is trying to retain his foothold in the Canfield house. (3) It introduces the train itself, which will reappear to play a role in the climactic chase sequence. (4) It introduces an element of suspense, since we are anxious to know what Willie will find on his return to the feuding South. (5) It is a way of establishing the geographical remoteness of the primitive South from civilised New York. (6) It is a means of establishing the historical remoteness of the pioneering period in which such feuding was possible. (The railway may also have had a sentimental significance for the Keatons. Joe Keaton had memories of the train on which he crossed from California to Oklahoma in 1892 or 1893; how the passengers had to keep getting off the train to pick up wood to feed its boilers.)

Keaton's treatment of period is here very much more sophisticated than in *The Three Ages*. The comic-strip anachronistic joke is almost abandoned except for a charming little gag when a rustic crossroads is described as 'Broadway and 42nd Street as it was in 1830. From an old print' (a gentle jibe at the source references that occasionally appeared in Griffith titles). Willie on his gentleman's hobby-horse is held up by a whiskery, high-hatted policeman while a buggy jogs by. The traffic cop rejoins his cronies on the street corner: 'This is getting to be a dangerous crossing.' Otherwise the film caricatures the quaintness of pioneer railroad days only with the subtlest sort of satire. 'Onward sped the iron monster;' but as the flimsy contraption rambles through the wilderness and the cattle stampede and the country people wonder, it could just as well be from a Ford film. The train *is* funny; but it is the funniness of the real thing. Keaton told John Gillett in 1965: 'All right, we say . . . let's look up the records and see when the first railroad train was invented. Well we find out: we've got the Stephenson Rocket for England and the DeWitt Clinton for the United States. And we chose the Rocket engine because it's funnier looking. The passenger coaches were stage coaches with flanged wheels put on them. So we built that entire train and that set our period for us. . . .' In other respects also the period staging is meticulous. Willie's costume, though his enormous hat is a rich source of comedy, is accurately in period and sensationally elegant. The absurd hobby-horse on which he makes his first appearance was, according to Keaton, begged afterwards by the Smithsonian, as a museum-class replica. Even more admirable is the way in which the staged period elements are assimilated into the natural settings—the breathtaking Sierra Nevada landscape, still untouched by the automobile age. The dainty little train seen in long-shot against the forests or half silhouetted as it crosses a dramatic high bridge becomes part of this landscape; and unforgettable.

All the elements of the film—the dramatic integrity of the action, the conscientious period reconstructions, the use of locations of striking visual beauty and grandeur—contribute to the logic and realism that Keaton was by now seeking as a basis for his comedy. The gags are all the funnier because they are sprung out of a realistic situation and tried against the touchstone of reality.

Perhaps nowhere else in all Keaton's work are we so strikingly aware of the combination of his gifts as performer, as *metteur en scène* and as film-maker. The studio-built waterfall on which much of the action was shot must have been in the region of fifteen feet high. 'We had to build that dam; we built it in order to fit that trick. The set was built over a swimming-pool, and we actually put up four eight-inch water pipes with big pumps and motors to run them, to carry the water up from the pool to create our waterfall. That fall was about six inches deep. A couple of times I swung out underneath there and dropped upside down when I caught her. I had to go to the doctor right there and then. They pumped out my ears and nostrils and drained me, because when a full volume of water like that comes down and hits you and you're upside down—then you really get it.' Willie performs prodigies—

struggling with a heavy log in the fast-flowing Truckee River, or doing reckless acrobatics on the end of his rope. The sequence, from Willie being hurled out of the floating railway tender to the couple driving off in the parson's chaise, is accomplished in something like fifty shots occupying most of the last reel:

1. L.S. River. Willie sails down in tender, is tipped out into rapids.
2. M.L.S. Willie, standing in the rapids, tries to pull loose the rope around his waist, which has caught in the rocks. Jerks himself over on to his back.
3. M.L.S. River; reverse of 2. Willie falling backwards into water.
4. L.S. River. Bank in foreground, with girl sitting on it. Willie floats by. Girl gets up and runs off in panic.
5. Pan shot of Willie as he floats down the river.
6. M.S. River. Willie shoots over rock.
7. M.S. River. Willie shoots over rock.
8. M.S. River. Willie is shot up out of the water and falls back again.
9. L.S. River bank. Girl gets into canoe and pushes off into stream.
10. L.S. River. Girl is swept in canoe downstream.
11. M.S. River. Willie, as he is swept downstream, grabs foliage on the bank and begins to pull himself up; but the foliage breaks off.
12. L.S. River. Girl in canoe is swept downstream towards rapids.
13. L.S. River. Girl is thrown out of canoe which sweeps on without her.
14. L.S. River. Empty canoe is swept by, followed by the helpless girl.
15. M.S. River. Willie, swept along by the tide, comes to a log to which he attaches the rope still tied round his waist. He sits astride the log which is swept loose and floats off downstream.
16. M.S. River. Willie is swept downstream, clinging to his log.
17. L.S. Brink of waterfall. Willie and the log are swept to the edge. The log catches in the rocks while Willie is swept over the edge and hangs swinging at the end of the rope. For a second or so he hangs, kicking his legs in the air.
18. M.L.S. Falls seen from reverse view, looking downstream over the brink. Beyond the falls a distant forest can be seen. Willie swings for a moment, then climbs up over the rocky edge and on to the ledge at the top.

19. L.S. The falls, seen from Willie's viewpoint: a veritable Niagara crashing on the rocks below.
20. M.L.S. Top of falls. Willie, clinging to his log, looks down again.
21. As 19.
22. As 20. Willie climbs on top of his log and thence to the ledge. He tries to pull the rope loose from the log; then to dislodge the log.
23. M.L.S. River. Girl being swept downstream.
24. M.L.S. as 22. Willie still struggling with rope looks down.
25. L.S. Falls. Willie struggles.
26. L.S. Falls. The girl's boat goes over the brink, watched by Willie.
27. As 19, 21. The boat crashes on the rocks below.
28. M.S. Top of falls. Willie, more agitated than ever, struggles to free himself.
29. M.S. River. Girl is helpless in the water.
30. M.S. Top of falls. Willie is by now frantic.
31. M.S. as 29.
32. M.S. Willie attacks rope with stone.
33. M.S. Girl, swept downstream, snatches hopelessly at foliage on bank.
34. L.S. Falls. Girl approaches the edge as Willie ineffectually signals her to go back. He scrambles to the edge.
35. M.S. Edge of falls. The girl approaches the brink.
36. L.S. Falls. Willie swings down over the edge of the falls on his rope and snatches the girl from the brink. They swing in the air. (In this shot alone the girl is replaced by a dummy.)
37. Closer shot of Willie and the girl swinging on the rope. Willie deposits the girl on a ledge a little below the top of the falls, and continues to swing.
38. M.S. Ledge. Girl crouches on ledge.
39. M.S. Willie swinging on rope. He climbs on to the upper ledge.
40. Closer shot. Willie gets on to the ledge and tries to release himself from the rope.
41. C.U. Water's edge. The log breaks loose.
42. As 40. The log breaks loose. Frantically Willie pulls on rope.
43. L.S. Falls. The log goes over the edge, breaking the rope.
44. M.S. Ledge on which girl is waiting. Willie joins her.
45. C.U. Willie and the girl going into a clinch.

46. M.S. A road. The parson gets out of his chaise and goes towards the river.
47. As 45. Willie and the girl look up.
48. As 47 but longer shot. The parson comes down the path towards Willie and the girl. Willie and the parson support the girl between them and go off up path.

In his previous films Keaton had revealed an ingenious talent for setting up gags in terms of the camera. Here however his highly developed gifts as a film-maker come into evidence. The exposition of the sequence is lucid and entirely pictorial (there are no titles whatsoever until the very end of the reel). The images are invariably correct and just and the rhythms impeccable. Keaton is not inclined to use the traditional post-Griffith techniques of cutting, which tended to a rather formal repetition of shots and set-ups, but prefers a freer style of *mise en scène* which is sometimes remarkably modern in feeling. This free style, owing nothing to contemporary conventions, contributes to the undated look of his films today.

The succeeding and final sequence reveals the economy and accuracy with which Keaton could develop a dramatic situation; and the deftness with which he can shift his mood from drama to comic bathos. It also includes one of the first examples of Keaton's Wellesian ability to use the screen three-dimensionally, setting off foreground action against action seen in the depth of the frame: in this case the girl's father pushes open a door to perceive, in the far background of the room within the door, his daughter and Willie in an embrace. Subsequently even this set-up is elaborated:

TITLE: 'DARKNESS PUT AN END TO THE FRUITLESS SEARCH'
52. L.S. Exterior house at night. Lights shining from windows.
53. Interior of house—the hallway. The Canfield boys enter the front door.
54. Interior of house—foot of stairway. Canfield senior walks across and is joined by his two sons.
TITLE: 'HAVE THE HORSES READY AT DAYBREAK'
55. As 54. The three men go upstairs.
56. C.U. Exterior door of girl's bedroom. Canfield knocks and pushes it open.

57. C.U. Exterior door, another angle. As it opens, Willie and the girl can be seen in the depth of the room in each other's arms.
58. C.U. Canfield boys outside the door.
59. As 57. The Canfield boys come up behind their father.
60. M.S. Reverse shot, looking out of the door as the three men draw their guns.
61. M.S. Interior of bedroom, the door to the right of the screen. Canfield enters the door, followed by his sons. As they push the door wider open, the parson is revealed behind it.
62. C.U. Parson.
63. As 61. The parson walks across and the sons join the group.
64. As 62.

TITLE: 'WON'T YOU KISS THE BRIDE?'

65. M.C.U. Canfield. He is astonished . . . then gradually puts his left hand over the barrel of his gun.
66. M.C.U. The girl, the parson, Canfield. The girl crosses in front of the parson to her father.
67. C.U. Father facing camera; girl in front of him with back to camera. He embraces her, and looks over her head at . . .
68. C.U. A framed text: 'LOVE THY NEIGHBOUR AS THYSELF'
69. As 67. Canfield strokes his daughter's head, kisses her and clasps her to him.
70. Full tableau group: Willie, Parson, Girl, Canfield, Canfield boys. Canfield extends his hand to Willie, then lays his gun on the table. The Canfield boys follow suit. Willie shrugs, and in his turn takes six guns out of his belt. As the girl goes towards him to embrace him, he remembers, and takes a further, very small pistol out of his boot.

TITLE: 'THE END.'

From shot to shot the action moves with admirable fluidity; and one of Keaton's favourite gags—the gradual revelation of a pictorial situation which he so often uses for the surprise openings of his films—is here used for dramatic surprise, as the door is quite casually pushed open to reveal that the parson is in the room with the young couple. How neatly, too, is the wall-text introduced, to avoid the need for more than the basic two titles in this sequence of quite elaborate psychological action. *Our Hospitality* shows Keaton in full possession of his mature gifts: as a film-maker he is as assured as a King or a Vidor; and certainly the superior of Chaplin, who at the time that Keaton was making *Our Hospitality* was preparing *The Gold Rush*—a beautiful film, but technically archaic and visually feeble when seen alongside the Keaton film.

7: *Sherlock Junior*

In *Sherlock Junior*, released in April 1924, Keaton permitted himself a certain licence in applying his principle that comedy must not be 'too ridiculous' by putting the film, like *Convict 13*, the first part of *The Playhouse*, and *The Love Nest*, into the framework of a dream. 'That was the reason for making the whole picture. Just that one situation: that a motion picture projectionist in a theatre goes to sleep and visualises himself getting mixed up with the characters on the screen.'

The first reel of the film establishes the real-life situation which will subsequently be fantasticated in the hero's dream. The Boy is a projectionist and sweeper-up in a neighbourhood cinema; and in off-duty hours a would-be amateur detective. The character is introduced in a characteristic Keaton series of openings-up: first we see him in close-up, wearing a large moustache and importantly examining finger-prints through a magnifying glass. Then the camera draws back to reveal that the finger-prints are on the back of a book called *How to be a Detective*. Then in mid-shot we see that he is sitting in a cinema seat and that in the aisle is a broom and a pile of rubbish. The cinema proprietor comes in and sets him about his work. Without a single title, then, we have a complete exposition of the fantasy and the reality of the hero's life.

Taking his girl a one-dollar box of chocolates (the best he can afford) he indulges in innocent show-off by altering the price on the box to read four dollars. His rival, a lounge lizard, meanwhile steals the girl's father's watch and pawns it in order to buy *his* present to her; and subsequently he plants the tell-tale pawn ticket in the hero's pocket. Thus framed, the hero is dismissed the house in disgrace. The indefatigable dick, he tails the villain (with predictably disastrous results to himself), though at the very moment that he returns disconsolate to his job as projectionist, the girl is discovering the truth about the crime from the pawnbroker.

The sequence that follows is among the most extraordinary in Keaton's films. At its simplest level it is an in-joke about the technique of editing film; and a reminder that Keaton, as the last reel of *Our Hospitality* so clearly shows, was far too good an instinctive film-maker to use editing for its own sake, as a good many of his contemporaries, post-Griffith directors, were in danger of doing. At another level it explores the surrealist principle that lies at the heart of the medium. The projectionist starts off his film, 'Veronial Film Company presents "HEARTS AND PEARLS" '; and then drops asleep on the stool beside his projector. As he sleeps his dream double rises up and looks through the projection-box window. On the screen the hero and villain have been metamorphosed into the real-life girl and villain of the framing story. Seeing the girl's honour threatened, and failing to arouse his sleeping other self, the dream hero rushes down the aisle, scrambles up over the orchestra pit and enters the screen world. He is promptly kicked off the screen by the villain. As he scrambles back once again, the image cuts, and he finds himself before a closed front door. As he goes up to the door, the image cuts again, and he is standing in a garden. As he tries to sit on the garden seat, it cuts to a busy street and he sits down backwards, somersaulting into the rushing traffic. He starts to walk along the street, but finds he is teetering on the edge of a precipice. Peering over the edge, he finds himself instead looking down into the mouth of a lion. Cautiously retreating from the lions' den, he finds himself in a desert. Narrowly missing death by a train which rushes suddenly through the desert track, he sits down on a cactus. He settles down on a hillock but the shot cuts to an island. Diving off into the sea, the scene changes to a snowscape and he lands head-first in a

Sherlock Junior: 'dismissed the house in disgrace' →

Sherlock Junior

snow-drift, legs kicking in the air. He stretches one arm out to lean against a tree, but falls over as the shot cuts back to the original garden scene.

This sequence has been seen on the screen of the cinema within the cinema screen. Now the camera moves in to exclude the cinema auditorium. The dream screen fills the whole of our screen, drawing us also into the dream. The girl's father announces that a diamond necklace has been stolen and that he has sent for Sherlock Junior, the great detective. The villain and his accomplice, the butler, reveal their preparations for the detective: an explosive billiard-ball and a booby-trapped chair. Sherlock Junior arrives and turns all their plots back on themselves.

The rest of the film is an alternating pursuit between Sherlock Junior and the villains, a mounting climax of chase and escape gags. Sherlock Junior escapes from a roof by swinging downwards on a pole-gate to drop accurately into the back of the villain's

Sherlock Junior

moving car. Subsequently he escapes from the villain's clutches by diving through a window in which he has previously placed a hoop-shaped flat box, containing a woman's dress and bonnet. In the moment of crashing through the hoop like a bareback rider in a circus, the disguise fits about him. Trapped by a dead end, he dives straight through a pedlar woman's tray and apparently disappears completely through her body (the pedlar woman is actually Sherlock Junior's assistant in disguise). A long solo ride on the handlebars of a motor-cycle (the driver, his assistant again, has fallen off without his passenger noticing) is a gag trajectory which ends with Sherlock Junior shooting feet-first through a window and into the chest of the wicked butler, to effect the girl's rescue. Their triumphant getaway in the villain's car is cut short when, braking suddenly on four-wheel brakes, the body of the car flies clear of the chassis and into a river. Resourcefully, Sherlock Junior raises the canvas hood to act as an improvised sail; but the car sinks with the serene inevitability of the 'Damfino' . . . and the projectionist wakens, just as the real-life heroine comes in to ask his forgiveness for the mistake they have made over the watch.

The sang-froid of the super-detective has quite deserted the hero now; and his hands—as so often when Buster has to face emotional crises—flutter about, searching for a resting-place. He looks, of course, to the screen for inspiration. The screen hero firmly turns the girl towards him and pats her head. Buster does the same. The screen hero kisses the girl's hands. So does Buster. The hero gives her a ring. So does Buster. A lingering, passionate kiss on the screen. Buster bestows a staccato peck. The screen fades out on a shot of the happy couple dandling three babies. Buster scratches his head.

Sherlock Junior is a virtuoso piece, displaying every facet of the skills which had now reached the peak of their development. We see the impeccable technique as a performer which came from years of industrious vaudeville study. Trailing the villain's heels (literally) in the framing story, Keaton duplicates every movement, every step or jump with uncanny precision; and a variation on this exact duplication, where the villain throws a cigarette butt over his shoulder and Buster delays it to take a puff before throwing it over *his* shoulder, produces a brilliant comic counterpoint effect. He was always prepared to add new skills to the ones already acquired. The billiard game in which the hero unerringly pockets all the balls was not faked. Keaton studied the table, and then set it up so that he could himself make the master strokes.

The trailing scene ends with a dazzlingly spectacular feat. The villain shuts him in the refrigeration wagon of a train. A moment later, Buster emerges from a trapdoor on top of the train. As the train begins to move off to the right, Buster walks along the top of the carriages to the left, the camera panning beautifully to keep him centre shot. He neatly jumps from carriage to carriage till he comes to the end of the train. Jumping off the end, he grabs the chain of an overhead water-feed (which we saw in use at the start of the shot, just as he was scrambling through the trapdoor). His weight brings down the feed, and as he hangs there a great torrent

Sherlock Junior

of water douses him, washing him on to the track. As he makes off
into the background, two men come along the track on a hand-
operated rail truck; and ride straight under the water spout. This
remarkable and flawless gag is contained *in a single shot* lasting
some forty seconds. Nothing in it could be faked; and in fact
Keaton, in falling to the track, fractured his neck, although he
continued working and only discovered the extent of the damage
in an X ray, years later.

The trajectory of the final chase moves with unflagging speed
and unfaltering rhythm from gag to gag. Fleeing from the
criminals, and running wildly along a road, the hero is overtaken
by a motor-cycle cop, who turns out to be his assistant. The assistant gives him a lift on the handlebars, but promptly falls off the
back as the bike hits a bump. Unaware that he is riding solo on
the handlebars, Sherlock Junior negotiates speeding traffic, upsets
a woman crossing the street with her bundles of washing; runs

along a line of ditch-digging navvies, each of whom flings a spade of dirt in his face; runs through an Irish merry-making, carrying off with him the tug-of-war teams as he tangles with their rope. The beautiful geometry of the sequence reaches its peak as the motor-cycle goes across a bridge under construction. As Sherlock Junior approaches a large gap in the bridge, two pantechnicons coincide beneath it, so that he can ride safely over their roofs. As he approaches the unfinished end of the bridge, the whole thing collapses, a squashed parallelogram, gently depositing him back on ground level. Racing along the road, he approaches a huge log which is obstructing the way; but workmen have just placed dynamite under the middle of the log which explodes, parting like the Red Sea. He drives straight through the middle of a vehicle of curious form; he just misses an express; and, putting his hands over his eyes, narrowly avoids a car without even seeing it.

At this desperate point he suddenly realises that the motor-cycle has no driver; and for the first time loses his nerve. The sequence ends with a tremendous, foreshortened, three-second climax:

1. M.S. Road. Sherlock Junior approaching camera on motor-cycle.
2. M.S. Gangsters' hut to right of screen. Sherlock Junior on motor-cycle enters from left, hits obstruction and is thrown through the window of the hut.
3. Interior of hut. Table centre; butler at right of it. Sherlock Junior shoots through window, across table and slams into butler.
4. M.S. gangsters' hut, now seen to left of screen. Butler bursts out through the wall.

'You know the scene in *Sherlock Junior* where I call a motor-cycle cop, jump on his handlebars, and we hit a bump in the street and I lose the cop,' Keaton told Kevin Brownlow. 'Well, the cop that fell off was me. I took Ernie Orsatti, an assistant prop man, who was my size—put my clothes on him and I put on the cop's clothes. Then I had to do the scene where I ride on the handlebars. That was a hell of a job. Number one, I've got no brakes—there are only footbrakes, see. Well, I got some beautiful spills, some real beauties! I parked right on top of an automobile once. I hit it head on. I ended up with my fanny up against the windshield, my feet straight in the air!'

As reported in interviews, Keaton, generally very precise in his recollections, gave slightly different versions of the techniques used to film the great sequence in which the scenes cut while the actor in them stays continuously from one to the other. He told Christopher Bishop: 'We built what looked like a motion picture screen and actually built a stage into that frame but lit it in such a way that it looked like a motion picture being projected on a screen. But it was real actors and the lighting effect gave us the illusion, so I could go out of semi-darkness into that well-lit screen right from the front row of the theatre right into the picture. Then when it came to the scene changing on me when I got up there, that was a case of timing and on every one of those things we would measure the distance to the fraction of an inch from the camera to where I was standing, also with a surveying outfit to get the exact height and angle so that there wouldn't be a fraction of an inch missing on me, and then we changed the setting to what we wanted it to be and I got back into that same spot and it overlapped the action to get the effect of the scene changing.' Shortly before his death, Keaton told John Gillett much the same thing: 'We used measuring instruments for that sequence. When I stood on that rock I was going to jump into the ocean, but as I jumped the sea changed to something else. As I looked down I held still for a moment, and we ended that scene. Then we brought out the tape-measures, put a cross-bar in front of the camera to square it off, and measured me from two angles. That made sure I was in exactly the same spot as far as the camera was concerned. We also used surveyor's instruments to get me the same height, so that when we changed the scene and I went back on the set I was in exactly the same place as in the first shot. Then the cameraman just starts to crank and I jump; and when I jump I hit something else. I don't remember what I hit, but I hit something. This was all done just by changing the sets. But I on the screen never changed.'

On the other hand, to Kevin Brownlow Keaton suggested that he had not, in fact, needed to use surveyor's instruments. 'All we needed on this was the exact distance and the cameraman could judge the height. As we did one shot we'd develop it there and then, cut out a few frames, and put them in the camera gate. With that as a guide, the cameraman could put me right square where I was. As long as the distance was correct. Every cameraman in the business went to see that picture more than once trying to figure out how the hell we did some of that. . . .'

8: *The Navigator*

Keaton's second 1924 film, *The Navigator*, was conceived entirely by chance, and in the great tradition of creating a whole comedy out of a single prop. 'Sitting around the studio with the scenario outfit between pictures, and we're all groping for an idea, and we happen to hit a rut and nobody could think of anything that looked worthwhile. But at that time Frank Lloyd was making a picture for Metro which was right across the street from our studio, called *The Sea Hawk*. I had a great technical man (Fred Gabourie) and they borrowed him from me and sent him up to 'Frisco to see if he could find any old four-masted schooner hulls. And while he was up there looking for these four-masted schooners, those that could be repaired enough to use—'cause Frank had to have four or five in a fleet or something like that for the picture—he found this ocean liner up there that they were going to salvage. It was called the *Buford*. It was the boat that brought the last princess over to this country from Russia, smuggled her out, I guess. And we found out that you could have this boat for twenty-five thousand dollars. . . . Buy it! Now it's an ocean liner, about five hundred feet long. A passenger ship. This was in '23. So the minute we heard that we set out to see what we could do with it. Well, we got our start. Our start was a pip. . . .' Keaton claimed that after the film was finished, the ship was sold back to the salvage firm for the cost price. The story was apparently Jean Havez' idea. A rich young couple, who have never needed to learn to look after

themselves, find themselves adrift together on a deserted liner where the ordinary difficulties of existence are magnified by the fact that all the amenities are intended not for individual needs, but to cater for a thousand people.

Buster's character of the young millionaire ('Rollo Treadway—heir to the Treadway fortune—a living proof that every family tree must have its sap') is a variation of the character of Bertie in *The Saphead* and Alfred Butler in *Battling Butler*. While Bertie, however, belongs in the tradition of the comic idiot—a tradition which to an extent embraces Harold Lloyd's character—in that he wins through in the end by luck and miracle, both Rollo and Alfred are extended by the circumstances into which the story puts them. From being effete, ineffectual and totally reliant on servants (Rollo even takes his car and chauffeur when he wants to cross the road) they develop out of themselves resources of energy and ingenuity. Miracles only play a tiny role.

Again, as in *Our Hospitality*, Keaton uses a serious dramatic prologue to provide the motive for a comic action. 'Our story deals with one of those queer tricks that fate sometimes plays. Nobody would believe for instance that the entire lives of a peaceful American boy and girl could be changed by a funny little war between two small countries far across the sea. And yet it came to pass. The spies of the two little nations were at a Pacific sea port, each trying to prevent the other getting ships and supplies.' A group of rather (but not too) hammy spies plot to set 'The Navigator' adrift under cover of darkness. Meanwhile on the other side of the city, Rollo is having the inspiration that he will get married. He therefore drives across the road to propose to the heroine, who lives with her millionaire father in the house opposite. She rejects him; and disconsolate but quite unsurprised, he returns home (leaving the car to do its U-turn without him; 'a long walk will do me good').

The girl's father is the owner of 'The Navigator.' That night, attempting to go aboard his ship, he is hijacked by the spies; and his daughter, intending to run to his assistance, succeeds in getting aboard the empty ship just as it is set adrift. In fact it is not quite empty. Rollo, off to Honolulu to forget his sorrows, has got the wrong pier (again Keaton uses the old trick of the half-covered notice: a partially opened gate obscures the 1 of 12; just as the flat revealed only the more enticing part of the theatre poster in *Back Stage*); and he also has boarded 'The Navigator.' Next day they meet after a chase of accelerating speed and panic round the decks of the deserted ship, during which they always manage to avoid crossing each other's path until Rollo falls down an air shaft, hat first, on to a seat beside the girl, to gasp out as his first words, 'Will you marry me?' Their first day is a nightmare of coping with domestic equipment meant for hundreds; their first night is a pantomime of scares and confusions.

Weeks later we find them still adrift, but ingeniously adjusted to the situation. They sleep in the insulated quiet of the ship's boilers; and the galley is a forest of levers and pulleys and wires, all the business of living neatly mechanised. A lever fills the coffee-pot with coffee and water and puts coals on the fire. A saw, improvised out of a grindstone and handsaw, opens tins and files Rollo's nails in one operation. A cage lowers eggs into the giant cooking pot which had earlier given such trouble; and a further series of levers and pulleys sets the table.

They sight land. Rollo realises first . . . and compassionately watches the girl's mounting terror as she too recognises that the island they see is occupied by cannibals. Drifting helplessly towards the island, they attempt to drop anchor, but the anchor fouls the propeller. Rollo bravely, if unwillingly, goes down in a diving-suit to release it. While he is having his troubles below water, the cannibals row out in their canoes, board 'The Navi-gator,' carry off the girl and sever the lines and air-pipes of Rollo's diving equipment. Rollo's appearance like some sprite out of the water temporarily routs the cannibals, and he and the girl regain the boat. The cannibals attack again; but Rollo's resourcefulness holds them off for a while. The end is a characteristic Keaton twist. He and the girl have finally taken to the water, and in a fatalistic embrace sink slowly beneath the waves . . . only to rise up again like Excalibur. A submarine has surfaced beneath them.

Inside the submarine, the girl kisses Rollo, who is so surprised that he falls into the vessel's controls, and turns the submarine upside down.

The variety of Keaton's films is constantly striking: he and his writers never repeated a structural formula. *The Three Ages* had its elaborate interweaving of three stories; *Our Hospitality* was a direct adventure story, given a comic orientation; *Sherlock Junior* is a dream within a dream, a surrealistically heightened detective adventure. *The Navigator* develops the personalities and relationships of its hero and heroine (alone for the greater part of the film) through a progressive series of self-contained comic sequences. With surprising neatness, the film divides into twelve clear-cut sequences:

1. The Spies' Plot.
2. Rollo Treadway at home.
3. The proposal.
4. Night: the accidents which get Rollo and the girl on to 'The Navigator.'
5. Morning: the chase around the decks and eventual meeting.
6. The difficulties of making breakfast.
7. A ship is sighted. In their excitement, both manage to fall overboard, with consequent complications.
8. Night: the problems of sleeping; various alarums, including the appearance of a sinister face at the porthole, which turns out only to be a photograph which the girl has thrown overboard but which has caught on a hook on the side of the ship; some exploding fireworks; the ghostly gramophone which suddenly starts to play 'Asleep in the deep'; the mysteriously swinging doors.
9. Weeks later—still drifting; but with the problems of living mostly solved: the boiler bedrooms; the automated galley.
10. The cannibal island sighted: Rollo's underwater adventure.
11. The fight with the cannibals on board ship.
12. Rescue.

Again, in *The Navigator* the whole range of Keaton's talents is extended. The battle with the cannibals contains some of his finest comic falls. The gags are so densely packed and so tightly interwoven that it is often hard to keep up with them or to recall their

111

sequence, in, for example, the galley scenes or the admirable sequence in which both Rollo and the girl manage to fall overboard and which ends with an entanglement with a collapsible chair which will do nothing *but* collapse. At the same time it is all organised with enormous dramatic skill; and the character of Rollo is developed with great logic and integrity. His growth from the spoiled fool of the opening to the resourceful hero of the end is perfectly credible. The stubborn imperturbability with which he joins battle with the cannibals is not in any way inconsistent with the sang-froid with which he makes his proposal to the girl and accepts the ensuing rebuff—coolly retrieving the hat and stick that he has a moment before deposited with the butler. The only time he is visibly startled out of his sang-froid is when *he* realises that the girl is about to realise that they have a diving-suit to hand and is liable to propose that he use it to release the anchor chain.

At the technical and mechanical level *The Navigator* is one of Keaton's most elaborate films. Even he could not have found a more elaborate prop than a liner; and it gave him some excellent gags. But even such a comparatively simple-looking effect as the row of cabin doors which open and shut in an eerie way as the ship rolls required a highly intricate working out: 'Well, you have to go to the top of the door and use thin enough wire that it can't possibly photograph, and control 'em all the length of the decks; so that one batch of men down here could pull 'em open, and a batch over here could close 'em. And then we put the camera on a tripod that has a big weight hanging down, so by a man standing there and moving that weight in a figure eight, the camera gives the impression of the ship rolling. Well, the only thing we have to make sure of is when they take the camera over to this side that the doors open and as it sways back the doors close. Well on the screen it looks like that boat went over to about a thirty-three-degree angle and back. And then I leaned in the opposite direction like you would normally walk on the deck of a rolling ship. When everybody got timed together with doors and cameras moving in the right direction, and me moving in the right direction at the same time, you got your scene.'

Keaton's willingness—sometimes it seemed more like a per-verse compulsion—to undertake enormous technical problems for the sake of a gag is perhaps nowhere more evident than in the underwater sequence. The diving-suit proved an exceptionally fruitful prop. Putting it on, he plods about the deck in his lead boots with ludicrous solemnity. Absent-mindedly he keeps a lighted cigarette in his mouth as the girl screws on the helmet; and his stricken face is glimpsed through a smoke-hazed helmet window. (This touch appears to have been suggested by an accident that actually happened on the set.) He collects together his unlikely equipment—a knife, pistols, toolbag and 'danger men at work' notice-board—then descends into the water with a stiff, brave little wave at the girl. All-concealing as the diving-suit may be, it fails entirely to disguise Keaton. There is never a moment's doubt as to who it is moving about in it, on short, jerky little legs and with stiff, busy arms sticking out slightly at an angle.

Underwater, the little figure sinks gradually down to land in a sitting position on the sea bottom. Groping around in the misty light, he erects his warning notice and a red lamp. He picks up a bucket, empties it and swills it out before washing his hands—all under water. A lobster attaches itself to his trousers: he detaches it and uses it as a pair of pincers. Attacked by a sword-fish, he tucks the creature under his arm and uses it as a rapier, to duel with another sword-fish that comes along. At this moment the cannibals who have boarded 'The Navigator' cut his lines. He pulls at them, and finding them slack, follows them through to their ends. Again, even in his diving-suit, Buster's look of blank surprise is explicit.

The possibilities of the diving-suit are by no means exhausted. On shore the cannibals are holding the girl captive, when suddenly, rising up from the deep like some sea monster, comes the diver. Christopher Bishop has pointed out Keaton's remarkable power of visualisation in making us—even though we are already familiar with Rollo's diving-suit—see it with the same fresh shock that the primitive tribesmen experience.

Still the diving-suit is not finished with. To get the girl back to the boat, Buster lies on his back in the water and floats while she sits atop him, paddling. Arriving at 'The Navigator,' his water-logged suit is too heavy for him to clamber up the ladder. In the most startling image of the film he faces the camera, and then seems to commit *hara-kiri* upon the belly of the suit which horrifyingly disgorges a great torrent of water. Thereupon, falling upside down, he empties the water from the lower portions of the diving-suit as well.

As remarkable as the ability to remain totally recognisable even under so opaque a disguise as a diving-suit, was Keaton's ability to maintain his delicate and elusive comedy through all the hazards and distractions of extreme technical difficulties; which, of course, he supervised. He described to Kevin Brownlow how the diving sequence was done: 'First of all, we thought we'd use that big tank down at Riverside. If we built it up, we could get five or six feet more water in the deep end. So they went down and built it up, put the water in—and the added weight of water forced the bottom of the swimming pool out. Crumbled it like it was a cracker. So we had to rebuild their swimming pool. . . . Next thing, we tested over at Catalina, and we found there was a milk in the water—the mating season of the fish around the island causes that. The moment you touch the bottom it rises up with the mud—rises up and blacks out your scene on you. Lake Tahoe is the clearest water in the world, and it's always cold because it's up a mile high, and that's an awful big lake. So we went up to Tahoe. I'm actually working in around 20 feet of water in that scene.'

'You imagine, we built this camera box for two cameras, a little bigger than this table square, with a big iron passage up to the top, with a ladder on the inside. It holds two cameras and two camera-men. It was built of planks and sealed good so there was no leakage. But it's wood, and there has to be added weight. Well, I added about 1,000 lbs to it. Now we find that the inside's got to be kept at the same temperature as the water outside. So we hang a thermometer out there so the cameraman looking through the glass can read it. And one on the inside. First thing in the morning, and the night before, we have to put ice in there, and then add more to make sure to keep the temperature of the camera box the same as the water on the outside so it won't fog up the glass. Either one side or the other will fog on you, see. The difference was that when two bodies are in there, the body heat means we have to add more ice immediately. So as you put the cameraman in, you roll more ice in. . . .'

'So there's the whole outfit, and me with that deep sea diving suit down there—and the cameraman says, "I'm too close. I want to be back further." I moved that camera box, I moved it. That's how much you can lift when you're down around 15 to 20 feet deep. The box must have weighed about 1,400 lbs, something like that, with two cameras, two cameramen, about 300 lbs of ice, another 1,000 lbs of weight—and I picked it up and moved it. I was one month shooting that scene. I could only stay down there about thirty minutes because the cold water goes through into your kidneys. After about a half hour you begin to go numb. You want to get up and get out of there.'

Of all Keaton's heroines, Kathryn McGuire in *The Navigator* and Marion Mack in *The General* have the most positive roles. The actual stories demand from them a greater participation, in that hero and heroine are thrown together in isolation; and in any case the two girls are unusually charming and funny. Kathryn McGuire has the same sweet dizziness as Marion Mack: when the castaways want to attract the attention of a passing ship, she runs up the prettiest flag she can see, which happens to be the quarantine signal. Making coffee, she meticulously counts four beans into a 100-cup coffee-pot of water. She faints, but comes round sooner than expected and unfeelingly walks off leaving Rollo still struggling to erect the insistently collapsible chair to support her. At the same time she has moments of refreshing tartness: the firm 'Certainly not!' with which she greets a proposal of marriage is exemplary. Rollo's relationship with her, once they are thrown into the intimacy of the ship, is very much the same affectionate exasperation as Johnnie Gray evinces for his Southern belle in *The General*.

Concerned to give a sufficient weight to his dramatic scenes,

Two Keaton directors: Donald Crisp with Roscoe Arbuckle

Keaton took on the British-born director Donald Crisp (who had worked with Griffith and whose acting performances had included Battling Burrows, in *Broken Blossoms*) as co-director. (Crisp's is the face in the menacing portrait that terrifies Rollo when it appears at his porthole.) The trouble was that Crisp became fascinated by the techniques of comedy. 'He turned into a gag man. He wasn't interested in the dramatic scenes, he was only interested in the comedy scenes with me. Well that we didn't want. But we did manage to pull the picture through all right.' So successfully, indeed, that *The Navigator*—totally unfaded today after forty-four years—was Keaton's biggest box-office success. According to Rudi Blesh it grossed more than $2 million on its initial release; and had cost $212,000.

9: *Seven Chances*

It is tempting to connect the central situation of *Seven Chances*—the hero pursued by an army of monstrous, man-eating women—with the growing resentment that Keaton seems to have been feeling at this time against the Talmadge matriarchy into which he had married; but in fact it was Joseph Schenck who had bought the property—along with a new director who was got rid of before he could begin work. *Seven Chances* was an old Belasco flop, written by Roi Cooper Megrue and originally produced on the stage in 1916. For Keaton it was 'the type of unbelievable farce I don't like' (quoted by Rudi Blesh). As worked over by Keaton's writers, Bruckman, Mitchell and Havez, however, it became an ideal vehicle; and even the comedian grudgingly acknowledged that they 'got a fair picture.'

The film opens with a cod romantic prologue that was originally filmed in colour. As season succeeds season—spring, summer, autumn, winter and spring again—and a diminutive Dalmatian puppy grows to massive size, the shy hero, Jimmie Shannon, stands at the garden gate with Mary Brown, too timid to declare his love. Jimmie is a partner in a firm of brokers desperately in need of money. When a lawyer (the first appearance with Keaton of Snitz Edwards, the diminutive Jewish comedian and a veteran Broadway character player) comes to tell him of an enormous legacy, Jimmie and his partner Billy assume that he must be a creditor so give him the slip and go off to their country club. He

(above and opposite) Seven Chances

finally catches up with them and explains the terms of the inheritance: Jimmie must be married by the evening of his twenty-seventh birthday. Today.

Jimmie rushes round and proposes to Mary; but when he artlessly explains the reason for his haste, she angrily rejects him; and by the time she has reconsidered, his telephone has accidentally been knocked off the hook and he is already making a disastrous round of proposals to the most likely prospects for marriage. These all fail; but Billy has a plan and tells Jimmie to be at the church at five that afternoon.

Billy's impetuous plan is to publish the story of the young heir's search for a wife in the front page of the papers. As five o'clock approaches and the exhausted Jimmie naps in the front pew of the church, the brides begin to arrive—first in ones and twos and then in their hundreds, monstrous women of all colours in billowing dresses and improvised bridal veils, arriving on bicycles, horses,

roller skates, in cars, trams and trains, running and walking, packing the church and blocking all the roads leading to it. Recognising the bridegroom, who leaps out of the window, they give chase, trampling all before them as they stampede through the town and out into the country with Jimmie pistoning on ahead.

The film as originally completed apparently ended here, fading on the chase—'a real dud, and we knew it.' Subsequently, however, Keaton's principle of previewing his films and then 'building up the highspots' came effectively into action. ' . . . I went down to the dunes just off the Pacific Ocean out at Los Angeles, and I accidentally dislodged a boulder in coming down. All I had set up for the scene was a camera panning with me as I came over the skyline and was chased down into the valley. But I dislodged this rock, and it in turn dislodged two others, and they chased me down the hill.

'That's all there was: just three rocks. But the audience at the preview sat up in their seats and expected more. So we went right back and ordered 1,500 rocks built, from bowling alley size up to boulders eight feet in diameter. Then we went out to the Ridge Route, which is in the High Sierras, to a burnt mountain steeper than a forty-five degree angle. A couple of truckloads of men took these rocks up and planted them; and then I went up to the top and came down with the rocks. That gag gave me the whole final chase, and it was an accident in the first place.' Of the shooting of the scene, Keaton told John Gillett: 'When I've got a gag that spreads out, I hate to jump a camera into close-ups. So I do everything in the world I can to hold it in that long-shot and keep the action rolling. When I do use cuts I still won't go right into a close-up: I'll just go in maybe to a full figure, but that's about as close as I'll come. Close-ups are too jarring on the screen, and this type of cut can stop an audience from laughing.' The whole sequence is an outstanding demonstration of the combination of Keaton's skills as *metteur en scène* and a fearless, not to say miraculous, performer. It is one of the great Keaton trajectories. The women have chased him across country; and the climactic sequence begins with a long-shot looking down a deep gully between two precipitous cliffs. As the women charge towards the camera through the gully, Keaton crosses the screen from left to right, and makes up the hillside. 'I know a short cut: we'll head him off'; and the women charge. In long-shot we see the top of a plateau, and Keaton running along it. He leaps a cleft in the rocks, then arrives at a sheer cliff-edge, just in time to catch hold of the top of a newly felled tree which brings him down to the valley, descending in a perfect arc. He comes to a forty-five-degree gravel slope which he descends in a rapid series of hair-raising somersaults. And then the landslide proper begins. Clearly it was impossible to plan this scene except in the broadest sense. The rocks once set in motion, Buster had to dodge and flee as best he could; and Lessley had to keep cranking. The result is divine. The chase is filmed in long-shot; a rear view of Keaton pursued by rocks; a side view; rear view; then a somewhat longer shot with the camera panning down the hillside with beautiful accuracy, keeping Keaton in centre shot as he runs diagonally down the mountain; a frontal shot; then a longer side view.

At this point a set-up gag shot is inserted. Buster climbs a tree to escape the rocks, but almost immediately a huge boulder crashes into the foot of the tree and uproots it, starting the chase all over again. Then a long shot from the side shows him taking shelter beneath a huge boulder which has stuck on the hillside. He is unaware that a landslide is piling up behind this rock ready for a violent renewal. At this point, just as the landslide begins again, the brides appear, mounting the hill. For a moment Buster is caught between two threats; but the terrified brides give way before the avalanche. Now Buster turns and faces the landslide, avoiding the rocks as they bounce off a bagatelle-board arrangement of pegs in the ground. And finally the avalanche seems to have ended. Having held his ground throughout the whole disaster, he turns and walks down the hill . . . and a tiny laggardly little stone fells him.

It is hard to believe that the original ending was a fade-out on the chase, for Keaton endings are invariably tidily linked with the beginnings; and it seems more likely that the brief, happy epilogue which now ends the film was in the original, previewed version also. Jimmie ends the chase with a perilous crossing of a railway and road, only to get caught by his coat, at the last moment, on the gate leading to Mary's house. Uprooting the gate, posts and all, he rushes into the house where the preacher is waiting to marry the young couple. The emotional tease that follows is probably lifted from the original play. It is after seven, so he has lost his inheritance. He therefore refuses to burden Mary with a penniless husband. She wants to marry him just the same; but he goes sadly outside the house, where he lifts his eyes from a dramatic gesture of despair to notice that the church clock still wants two minutes of seven. He springs into activity, rushes inside; and they are married. There is a wry little pay-off: everyone—even the now monumental Dalmatian—wants to kiss the bride; and the groom cannot get near her.

Despite Keaton's doubts about *Seven Chances*, the film contains some memorable scenes quite apart from the landslide. The way in which he builds up the tempo of individual sequences is impeccable. The first of his series of unsuccessful proposals is greeted by loud and helpless laughter from the recipient: from this point the sequence builds up in pace and absurdity, heightened by subsequent encounters, progressively briefer in duration, with the first girl, still madly laughing. For this sequence he used a number of very charming and witty actresses (most of them sporting Louise Brooks hairdos) of which the most enchanting is a sardonic hat-check girl, who refuses before he even asks her, and gets very caustic and possessive over the tip which he gives and takes back as he suffers a certain indecision as to whether or not he intends to check his hat. The pile-up of brides in the church is equally skilful in its timing and build-up from the desultory arrival of the first one or two to the wild stampede. The women raze a cornfield, flatten two rugby teams who happen to be in their path, commandeer a bus by flinging out crew, passengers and all; and entirely demolish a newly built brick wall in order to provide themselves with missiles.

Keaton's skill as a *metteur en scène* is evident even in so simple a scene as that in which Mary is trying to telephone Jimmie to tell him that she has repented of her refusal to marry him. It has the simple mastery of a Mamoulian. We have seen Jimmie dislodge the receiver by pushing the telephone out of his way and *towards the camera*; and as the scene cuts between the girl at her telephone and the group of men in the office, discussing Jimmie's plans to find another bride, the telephone is always, characteristically, in the forefront of the shot. There is, too, a nice little refinement of the cutting gag in *Sherlock Junior*, now adapted to provide a brilliant linking device. When he drives from his office to Mary's house, and later back again, Jimmie sits in his car, but never moves off the spot. Only the background dissolves, to transfer him from one location to another. It is a charming and quite unstressed joke; and was not accomplished without effort: '. . . the other thing where I had to use surveyor's instruments . . . I had an automobile like a Stutz-Bearcat roadster. I was in front of an office building. Now it's a full figure shot of that automobile and me. There's a lot of people walking up and down the side-walks. I come down into the car, release the emergency brake after starting it, sit back to drive —and I don't move. The scene changes and I'm in front of a little cottage in the country. I reach forward, pull on the emergency brake, shut the motor off, and go on into the cottage. Later, I come out of the cottage, get into the automobile and the scene changes back to the city. I and the automobile never moved. Now that automobile has got to be the same distance, the same height and everything to make the scene work. For that baby, we used surveying instruments so that the front part of the car would be the same distance from the camera—the whole shooting match.'

10: *Go West*

In *Seven Chances* there is one of the small in-jokes of which Keaton was fond (another is the baseball team register which is seen in the modern sequence of *The Three Ages* and which includes the names of all the Keaton studio employees). When Snitz Edwards, as the lawyer, runs downstairs in pursuit of Jimmie and Billy, he bumps into a fat man, rather like John Bunny, on the landing. The fat man was in fact Jean Havez, one of Keaton's three gag-writers. As it happened, *Seven Chances* was the last film on which the team of Havez, Clyde Bruckman and Joseph Mitchell, who had all been with Keaton since the shorts period, worked. Bruckman went off to be a director, and to work for Harold Lloyd. Later he co-directed *The General* and rejoined Keaton as a writer in the years when both men were in the Hollywood wilderness. When in 1955 he committed suicide, it was with a gun borrowed from Keaton. Havez and Mitchell never worked with him again.

No explanation of the break-up is forthcoming; but to judge from the two films that followed, Keaton may well have missed the team, who seem always to have worked together with enormous gusto and proven success. *Go West* and *Battling Butler*, for all their individual qualities, have not nearly the attack and invention and assurance of *The Navigator* and *Seven Chances*. The gags are, for Keaton, thinly spread; and there seems not to have been the same heart for acrobatic miracles. At the same time *Go West* is

Go West: 'When you say that — smile'

one of Keaton's most endearing films. It is unique as the only
picture in which the comedian deliberately aimed at pathos; and
though it is totally unexpected in him and he never tried it again
to the same degree, he brings it off without the least embarrassment or mawkishness. What led him to this temporary deviation
we shall now never know. *Go West* was a film about which he
seems to have talked little in his old age, except to recall his happy
relations with the nice little cow who was his leading lady.

Keaton calls his own character 'Friendless.' An opening shot of
a statue of Horatio Alger with the inscription 'Go West, young
man' is followed by a title: 'The social standing of a certain young
man kept him continually on the move.' Friendless is first seen
hauling his bed, with all his possessions piled on it, to sell at the
general store. The storekeeper offers him one dollar sixty-five for
the whole lot, but takes back most of that when Friendless retrieves
his toilet articles from the drawer of a chest. With them is a

Brown Eyes and Friendless →

cherished photograph of his mother, which is referred to again once or twice in the course of the film. With the few pennies that remain, he buys a loaf of bread and a sausage, whose dwindling proportions provide a useful time device as Friendless journeys westwards, stealing rides on cross-continental freight trains. After spectacular adventures with some barrels in a freight wagon, he is forcibly deposited in the desert. He makes his way to a ranch, where he gets work; but his ineptness at the jobs he is given attracts the scorn and derision of his fellow cowboys. His first and only friend is Brown Eyes, a little heifer who is like him, ostracised and unloved. He takes a stone from her hoof; she shows her gratitude by saving him from an angry bull. They become inseparable; and Brown Eyes and Friendless protect each other. When he sees her being bullied by bigger cattle, he steals for her a set of deer antlers which he fixes to her head. When it is her turn for branding, he surreptitiously takes her aside and 'brands' her with his razor and shaving brush, using her milk instead of water for the operation. Meanwhile he also falls in love with the rancher's daughter.

The rancher resolves to send his cattle to the Los Angeles stockyards, and refuses to except Friendless' only companion. Friendless accompanies Brown Eyes on the cattle truck; and when the train is ambushed he is the only human being left aboard the train which, driverless, careers across the desert. Arriving in Los Angeles, Friendless looses the cattle which thereupon wander the city, terrorising the populace and causing chaos. Finally however, Friendless devises a ruse to control them. He dons a scarlet devil costume, and all the cattle pursue him as he runs faster and faster through the streets. (From time to time Keaton had used sound gags in silent films; here he is using a colour gag in a black and white film.) He arrives at the stockyards just in time to hand over the cattle to their relieved owner. 'My home and anything I have is yours for the asking,' says the rancher. 'I want her,' says Friendless, pointing. It is another example of Keaton's favourite surprise gag of only gradually revealing a visual situation. He is pointing, not as we and the rancher first suppose, at the girl, but at Brown

Eyes. As the film ends the four of them are driving off into the distance, Brown Eyes and Friendless cosy in the courting seat at the back of the car.

Whatever Keaton did he did conscientiously—even the sentimentality which was completely alien to him. Friendless' solitude and ostracism are constantly emphasised, by the photograph of his mother which he carries, by the harshness of the dealer, by the dog which simply walks away when Friendless tries to pat him, by the sadly comic little sequence in the big city where he is shoved and pushed and eventually walked over by the rushing crowds on the sidewalk. The most sentimental moment in all Keaton's work—certainly no less moving than the ending of *City Lights*—is when he recognises Brown Eyes' friendship. She has just saved him from the steer. Gratefully he gives her a tiny, cautious pat, and raises his hat. When she continues to follow him, he gazes at her, his face immobile, as much bewildered as touched by this unfamiliar affection.

The gags one recalls from the film are not the feats and marvels and extravagant inventions of *Our Hospitality* or *Sherlock Junior*, but quiet and charming little gestures: the politeness with which he raises his hat to Brown Eyes; the absurd little gun which he finds on a railroad siding early on in the film and which keeps reappearing throughout his cowboy career (it is always mislaying itself in the depths of a man-size holster until he has the inspiration of putting string on it like a baby's gloves); the step-ladder he fixes so that he can mount his horse; the minute calf which he cautiously selects as his contribution to the round-up, but which nevertheless foils all his attempts to lassoo it.

The finale, with the herd of cattle packing and panicking the streets of Los Angeles, is full of pleasant tricks—the men stampeded out of the Turkish bath; the frightened barber who shaves a path clean through his customer's hair; the Negro barber who leaps to safety over a partition only to find himself on the back of a steer; the dozing customer waiting for a shave who is fondly licked by a cow; the store customers who ride to safety on the overhead cash railway; the calf preening itself in the window of a

Go West: waiting for delivery, and parking

modiste's. Compared with the classic Keaton chase finales, however, it lacks structure and organisation. Keaton himself seems to have been keenly aware of this: his problem was the difficulty of controlling the tempo of the performances of the cattle, particularly since he dared not speed up their stampede in case it got out of control and became actual. The chase did, however, produce one of the cinema's great surrealist images: the line of policemen hanging on to one another's coat-tails, the first one hanging on to the devil's tail—the whole cortège pursued by bewildered bulls.

11: *Battling Butler*

Keaton often claimed that *Battling Butler* was his favourite film, though on other occasions, more credibly, he preferred *The Navigator* and *The General*. In the early scenes of the film, Keaton's comedy is at its most genial; but in the later reels the quality of pathos which appeared in *Go West* seems to have turned sour, to something very like masochism, particularly in the prolonged sequence in which Buster as the soft little rich boy is thrust into a brutal fight with the coarse and pitiless world champion boxer. The quality may simply be accidental. Keaton had clearly an understandable pride in his physical prowess (perhaps heightened by a consciousness of his small stature), and an against-the-odds boxing bout would be as natural a way as any in which to show it. Nevertheless this is possibly the least attractive of all Keaton's features.

He had himself bought the play, a Broadway success by Stanley Brightman and Austin Melford. It was adapted by a team of writers: Paul Gerard Smith, Al Boasberg, Charles H. Smith and Lex Neal. (Keaton remembered that Boasberg 'Had been a terrible flop when he tried to do sight gags for us. So were a hundred other writers we imported from New York. It is possible, of course, that we kept sending for the wrong ones.') Alfred Butler is a spoilt young man, not unlike Bertie in *The Saphead* and Rollo in *The Navigator*. But he is neither so incorrigibly senseless as the first, nor as resourceful as the second. He wins through less by ingenuity than by reason of a certain indecisiveness on the one hand, the doggedness of his love for the heroine on the other.

The film opens with Alfred's father sending him off, against the wishes of his doting mother, to the mountains, where he hopes a bit of shooting, fishing and hunting will make a man of him. Alfred drives off in his Rolls, with his valet, his wardrobe and camping equipment that includes a brass bedstead and running hot and cold water. His sporting activities are hopeless; and his attention is distracted by a beautiful young mountain girl. In the same matter-of-fact way of Rollo Treadway's courtship, Alfred instructs his valet to arrange a marriage with the mountain girl. When the valet's proxy proposal is received with derision by the girl's rugged family, the valet rashly boasts that despite all appearances, Alfred is really the world light-weight championship contender (who happens to have the same name).

Now Alfred has to live up to his reputation, which is only enhanced by the real Battling Butler's conquest of the world title. (There is a fascinating incidental glimpse of the period in the scenes of the girl's family listening to the fight on radio.) Poor Alfred is forced to persist in his pose; and when he meets the real prize-fighter, Battling Butler agrees to keep up the deception so that Alfred's girl friend shall not be disillusioned. In reality, however, Battling is intent on revenge for a fancied flirtation between Alfred and Battling's wife. He leads on the terrified Alfred to believe that he is to take the champion's place in a challenge contest with the Alabama Murderer. Even while the fight is actually on, poor Alfred is waiting in the dressing-room, due, as he supposes, to be called to his fate at any moment. After winning the fight, Battling comes to Alfred's dressing-room and proceeds to beat him up. Anger and love, however, give Alfred unwonted strength. He ends up laying out the champion. Triumphantly he takes his girl—now undeceived but still more proud of him—through the city streets. He is wearing a top hat, frock-coat, swagger cane—and boxer shorts.

As a straight dramatic film, in terms of *mise en scène*, *Battling Butler* has much to recommend it; and perhaps its comparative

Battling Butler, with Sally O'Neil →

weakness as a comedy actually affords us a better chance to assess with detachment just how good Keaton was at telling a story in film terms. The opening scene again employs a Wellesian deep-focus technique. In the foreground of the scene, in front of a door, Alfred's parents discuss their son. Through the door, in the depth of the scene, we can see the subject of their conversation, eating his breakfast, attended by a page and his valet who carefully smooths a misplaced hair on Alfred's head and knocks the ash off his cigarette for him. Later in the film there is a tricky compositional device in a reverse cut of Alfred, sparring with a great bruiser in the training ring, and looking through his opponent's crooked arm to see his wife at the ring-side with Battling Butler. If the story is unlikely and even unpleasant, at least it is stylishly told.

There are nice touches of character. Alfred gives a lift in his Rolls to Mrs Battling Butler. When he draws down a blind to protect himself from the sun, she coyly misunderstands and shoots it up again, defensively. Later Mrs Battling (handsomely decorated with a black eye by her jealous husband) happens to sit at the same table as Alfred's girl in the hotel garden. When a waiter brings a box of chocolates, 'with the compliments of Mr Butler,' the growing awareness of each other's sense of proprietorship in them and the consequently mounting jealousy and antagonism is acutely observed.

Keaton's own best scenes are mostly early in the film. Arriving at his mountain camp he goes shooting and peers myopically around while the rabbits and deer and other game play merrily about him. When his gun goes off by accident, it riddles the handkerchief in the hand of the passing mountain girl: 'Isn't she pretty' observes the oblivious Alfred to his valet as the girl hurls first abuse and then rocks at the two of them. The duck-shooting sequence that follows this remained one of Keaton's favourite pieces of business, and he continued to perform it on television to the end of his life. Drifting along in a tiny canoe, Alfred pulls out his gun in order to shoot a very infant duck, which thereupon vanishes under the water. When it reappears on the opposite side of the boat, Alfred loses his paddle and is obliged to use his rifle

Battling Butler: Snitz Edwards as the valet

in its place. When the duck reappears on the other side again, Alfred, slightly maddened, swipes at it with the gun. Peering into the water over the prow of his canoe, he capsizes the boat. At the moment when he has sunk until only his head is sticking out of the water, the girl passes by. Alfred politely raises his hat.

Alfred is a beautiful simpleton—which is perhaps why his transmutation, even under the influence of love, into a furious fist-fighter lacks conviction. After entertaining her to dinner, he walks the girl home. Then she has to walk him home, because he doesn't know the way. His proposal is made under difficulties: he is unaware that the girl thinks he is the prize-fighter. There is a frantic communication by signs between Alfred and his loyal valet behind the girl's back, from which Alfred can only suppose that the valet is recommending him to wallop the girl. At this point the resourceful Snitz Edwards gets him to one side with a nonchalant murmur of 'Sir, it's time to take your liniment.'

12: *The General*

Once when Keaton was asked why he thought *The General* looked so much more authentic than *Gone With the Wind,* he pondered for a moment and then replied with complete modesty, 'Well, they went to a novel for their story. We went to history.' The story is based on a curious reminiscence of the Civil War, William Pittenger's *The Great Locomotive Chase,* in which the author, a Northern soldier, recalled a daring raid in which he had taken part in 1862. A party of twenty men, led by one James J. Andrews and disguised as Southerners, made their way from Tennessee into Atlanta, and seized a train while its passengers were at breakfast. Their object was to run the train north to Chattanooga where they would join up with Union troops, having burnt bridges and cut communications along the route. Despite delays, they were within only a few miles of their destination when the crew of the train, on a borrowed locomotive, overtook them and forced them to abandon their prize. Most of the party were apprehended and several were executed.

The train and the chase were obvious attractions to Keaton; and this story gave him the weight of dramatic motive which he always sought in his comedy subjects. The major change he made was to see the story from the point of view of the Southern pursuers. 'You can always make villains out of the Northerners, but you cannot make a villain out of the South.' He considered that this was 'the first mistake' that Disney made when, more than thirty years

(*Above and opposite*) *The General*

afterwards, he adapted the adventure and called it by its original title. The other obvious advantage of his change of viewpoint is that it enables his heroes to end up on top—always an advantage in comedy.

Keaton's hero is Johnnie Gray, the engineer of the Western and Atlantic Flyer's locomotive. 'He has two loves in his life': his locomotive, 'The General,' and his girl Annabelle Lee. He is with Annabelle Lee when news comes of the attack on Fort Sumter. He is the first to enlist; but is refused by the board because as an engineer he is more useful to the Southern cause. But neither he nor Annabelle's family know the reason for his rejection; and his girl shuns him as a coward.

A year later, Annabelle Lee is to travel on Johnnie's train to visit her father, who has been wounded. She still will not even speak to Johnnie. But when the train stops at Big Shanty, the Northern spies hijack it, with Annabelle still aboard. Thus galvanised by the loss of both his loves in one and the same moment, Johnnie, single-handed, goes off in pursuit of the train—on a manual rail trolley; on a penny-farthing; on a borrowed train, with a cannon in tow. He has trouble with the cannon which persistently aims at him rather than at the enemy; with obstacles on the track; with the axe with which he tries to cut firewood. Absorbed in these problems he does not notice that he has penetrated the enemy's lines.

Entering the house where Annabelle is held captive, he overhears the enemy's plans to launch a surprise attack next morning. He rescues the girl and next morning manages to steal back 'The General.' Now the chase is reversed, with the Union soldiery after Johnnie. Along with Johnnie and Annabelle in the cab of 'The General' is a real general, a Northern officer who was knocked out in the struggle for possession of the locomotive. Crossing the Rock River Bridge, where the enemy forces plan to meet up, Johnnie sets it on fire behind him.

He reaches Southern field headquarters and warns them of the impending attack. In the rush to draw up an ambush to meet the enemy, Johnnie is left behind, struggling with a sword with a rather loose hilt and an over-tight scabbard which he has acquired on the way. Meanwhile the Union troops have reached the burning bridge. In illustration of Cocteau's *mot* that 'a good general will never give way—even to the facts,' the Union general cries: 'That bridge is not burned enough to stop you. My men will ford the river.' He is wrong of course: as the train moves on to the bridge, it collapses, hurling the locomotive into the ravine below, with great geysers of water and steam as it hits the river—perhaps the most spectacular of all slapstick catastrophes. The Confederate troops, having formed up in ambush on the opposite bank, open fire.

Johnnie, now in the Confederate front line, is having serious difficulty with his sword, still stuck determinedly in its scabbard. The anxious enthusiasm with which he tries to encourage the cannoneers turns to bewilderment as one by one they are picked off by a sniper. His last attempt to pull out his sword in a flourish of generalship frees it with such a jerk that while he holds the hilt

The General: an army passes unobserved

in his hand, the blade flies through the air to impale the sniper just as he is taking a bead on Johnnie. The sole survivor now, he fires the cannon, which with the devilry of any gun in Keaton's hands, suddenly aims itself straight up in the air. Keaton gets clear as briskly as he can: the ball comes down not on the enemy but on a dam which, being broken, launches a terrible flood which washes away the remainder of the Union forces.

Johnnie comes marching home on the fringe of the victorious Southern army. Running to inspect his locomotive, he finds the forgotten Union general just coming to in the cab. He hands over his prisoner, and is rewarded with a commission. At the fade-out he is seen sitting on the side of his engine, Annabelle Lee in one arm, the other fixed in a permanent salute in honour of the constant stream of soldiers who pass by.

The General is unique and perhaps perfect. In form and method it is like no other comedy, not even another Keaton picture. Here, uniquely, the dramatic action and the comic business are one and interdependent. You never feel that the story is simply an excuse for the comedy, or that the gags are a decoration planted on the story. Keaton was typically vague and modest about the way his films acquired their characteristic and striking visual qualities (even *The Frozen North* makes much more of its snowscapes than the much more ambitious *The Gold Rush*). He said that he always chose the actual camera set-ups 'when it was important for the scene I was going to do. If I had an incidental scene—someone runs in, say, and says "here, you've got to go and do this"—the background wasn't important. Then I generally just told the cameraman that I had these two characters in the scene, two full-length figures, and asked him to pick a good-looking background. He would go by the sun. He'd say, "I like that back crosslight coming in through the trees. There are clouds over there right now, so if we hurry up we can still get them before they disappear." So I would say "Swell," and go and direct the scene in front of the cameraman's set-up. We took pains to get good-looking scenery whenever we possibly could, no matter what we were shooting.'

Not even *Our Hospitality* is more beautiful than *The General*.

Every shot has the authenticity and the unassumingly correct composition of a Matthew Brady Civil War photograph. Keaton never considered the matter: he just assumed that whatever he did must be as authentic—visually as well as psychologically—as possible. 'In *The General* I took that page of history and I stuck to it in all detail. I staged it exactly the way it happened. . . . And I staged the chase exactly the way it happened.' He had originally wanted to use the original historical locations that Pittenger and his companions traversed sixty-five years earlier. In fact, though, Keaton had to use the breathtaking pine forests and mountains of Oregon, where there was still narrow-gauge railway track on which to run the two ancient locomotives he had found and converted to the authentic appearance of 1860's trains. His insistence that they should be powered by steam engines and fuelled with wood resulted in a forest fire in the course of shooting. Even the women's clothes (always a pitfall for art directors) were so accurate that you do not even notice them; and of course Keaton's own clothes— even to the coarse textures of the woollen cloth of his calling suit —are straight out of a daguerreotype. So, as James Agee pointed out, was his face.

He was totally uncompromising. If he was to show armies then he must have armies; and he appears to have used the entire Oregon State Guard for his war scenes. No one—not even Griffith or Huston and certainly not Fleming—caught the visual aspect of that war as Keaton did in the scenes of the railway marshalling yard and the ambush at Rock River. Just how uncompromising he was is evidenced by the astonishing scene of the collapsing bridge and the locomotive that crashes perhaps thirty feet into the water. It is said that the engine still lies there to this day, immovable.

A film built around trains was of course the culmination of a lifetime's fascination. 'Well, the moment you give me a locomotive and things like that to play with, as a rule I find some way of getting laughs out of it.' *The General* is an anthology of the greatest gags ever devised about railway trains. There is inevitably Keaton's favourite with pursued and pursuer diverging on to parallel tracks and joining up again in reverse order. Inevitably, too, there is a

'We'll dirty ours up a bit . . .'

water-feed. There is a variation on a joke from *Our Hospitality*
when Johnnie, having run out of fuel, passes under a bridge on
which the enemy are positioned. They pelt him with logs, which he
gratefully retrieves to stoke his boilers. For a fade-out to the first
sequence of the film Keaton devised a gag whose exquisite
simplicity was, as usual, hard won. He sits down on the driving-
bar of his locomotive, which begins to move, carrying him off as
his motionless body describes a complex series of arcs. 'Well, the
situation of the picture at that point is that she says, "never speak
to me again until you're in uniform." So the bottom has dropped
out of everything, and I've got nothing to do but sit down on my
engine and think. I don't know why they rejected me: they didn't
tell me it was because they didn't want to take a locomotive
engineer off his duty. My fireman wants to put the engine away in
the round-house and doesn't know that I'm sitting on the cross
bar, and starts to take it in.'

'. . . and let them have some rough treatment'

'I was running that engine myself all through the picture: I
could handle that thing so well I was stopping it on a dime. But
when it came to this shot I asked the engineer whether we could
do it. He said, "There's only one danger. A fraction too much
steam with these old-fashioned engines and the wheel spins. And
if it spins it will kill you right then and there." We tried it out four
or five times, and in the end the engineer was satisfied that he
could handle it. So we went ahead and did it. I wanted a fade-out
laugh for that sequence: although it's not a big gag it's cute and
funny enough to get me a nice laugh.'

In *The General*, however, it is less the gags you remember than
the image of the lonely, brave, beautiful, foolish little figure in
relentless pursuit of the two things which he loves most and which
have been stolen away from him. His relationship to both is
passionate and touching. When he is carried off on the driving-bar
he has become a part of his machine. And his relationship with

The General

Marian Mack is beautiful. The poor girl was roughly handled: at one point she is bundled into a sack and flung around with the freight. ('Oh God, that girl . . . had more fun with that picture than any film she'd made in her life. I guess it's because so many leading ladies in those days looked as though they had just walked out of a beauty parlour. They always kept them looking that way —even in covered wagons, they kept their leading ladies looking beautiful at all times. We said to thunder with that, we'll dirty ours up a bit and let them have some rough treatment.') Rescued, her attempts to help Johnnie are feminine and charmingly futile. When the fuel situation is desperate, she rejects a log with a knot in it and throws it overboard; then she hands up a tiny pencil-like chip that seems to her more pleasing. In the heat of the chase, she decides to tidy and sweep out the cab. Johnnie, exasperated, grabs her and shakes her violently—and then suddenly plants a tiny quick kiss on the face. It is a moment that reveals in a flash the tenderness and comedy and depth of Keaton.

13: *College*

Keaton was to make two more films as his own producer, but already the pressures of a changing and less free film industry were closing in on him. Lou Anger, the former Dutch comedian who had introduced him to Roscoe Arbuckle the day Arbuckle had 'invited him to come on down to the studio Monday' and had been Keaton's business manager ever since, had been taken by Schenck for the job—at this moment especially vital—of opening up exhibition outlets for United Artists throughout the country. Anger was replaced by Keaton's former publicity man, Harry Brand, who (presumably with the backing of Schenck himself) exercised his role of supervisor seriously. Keaton for the first time found himself subjected to producer interference.

On *College* Keaton had a new co-director, James W. Horne, who was subsequently to work over a long period with Laurel and Hardy. His writers were Carl Harbaugh and Brian Foy; and the distinct change of comedy style is emphasised by a different visual quality (though both Bert Haines and J. D. Jennings had worked with him before). The shift to a contemporary and familiar setting imposed a plainer pictorial style than in practically any other Keaton feature.

The conventional comedy structure—in story outline it might be a film by Lloyd or practically any other feature comedian—is in marked contrast to the highly individual form of *The General*. Keaton plays Ronald, a bookworm and mother's boy. Mary, the

College: spare-time soda-jerk

most popular girl in the school, prefers the athletic bone-head Jeff Brown. When Mary and Jeff go to Claydon College, Ronald, whose mother cannot afford the fees, decides to work his way through in order to be near the girl. He also resolves to turn himself into an athlete; and arrives at college with a trunkful of equipment and a series of teach-yourself athletics guides. His appearances on the baseball field and athletic track are disastrous. He confides to the Dean (the excellent Snitz Edwards again), who is distressed by the change in his favourite pupil's interests and the consequent falling-off in his academic work; and the kindly old gentleman tries to help him by forcing Ronald as cox on the college crew. Despite efforts to slip him a mickey finn, Ronald reports for the big boat race. The boat is called, inauspiciously, 'The Damfino.' Ronald heartily leaps into it, and goes straight through the bottom. The replacement boat is called 'Old Iron Bottom.' Halfway through the race, the rudder comes off; but

Ronald—inspired by a vision of Mary's encouraging face—ingeniously straps the rudder to his behind and steers by hanging his seat off the end of the boat.

Meanwhile the awful Jeff Brown has locked himself with Mary in her room, intent on getting her expelled along with himself. As Ronald, having coxed his crew to victory, is sitting in the changing-room, the telephone rings: it is Mary calling for help. The call of love launches Ronald into one of the most fierce and rapid Keaton trajectories, in which he miraculously masters all the athletic skills that had eluded him on the sports field. He hurdles a row of garden hedges, long-jumps a stream and uses a clothes-post to vault into the window of Mary's room.* Thereupon he assails the villainous Jeff with all sorts of missiles hurled with the precision of the discus; and uses a standard lamp like a javelin. The dean and the principal of the girl's college burst in. 'Young lady, do you know what this will mean?' 'Yes: it means we are going to be married.' And Ronald and Mary leave by the fire-escape. There is a coda, as macabre as the end of *Cops*. We see the happy couple going into church and, after a dissolve, coming out. We next see them as a middle-aged couple; then as a very aged Darby and Joan. And finally, a shot of two gravestones, side by side. It is in such a strange way that Keaton imposes his taste for the melancholy on a film whose tone is entirely optimistic.

Much less satisfying as a whole than *The Navigator* or *The General*, the compensations of *College* lie in the richness of its gags. It is as prolific as the shorts. At the graduation ceremony with which the film begins, Ronald's fifteen-dollar suit and his umbrella cause him excruciating embarrassments. Arriving in the hall with his mother (Florence Turner, once 'The Vitagraph Girl': this was among the last film roles of one of the first film stars), he cannot get his umbrella to go down. The man in the next seat obligingly does it for him, not without exasperation. Naturally Ronald cannot help himself experimenting, putting the umbrella up again to see if he can do it this time. He cannot, of course. The

---

* This was the only time Keaton ever used a double: the Olympic champion Lee Barnes from U.S.C.

College

suit shrinks, with a firing-off of buttons in all directions. 'What would I be without my book,' he orates as he hastily covers his fly-front with a handy volume.

Working his way through college, he gets a job as a soda-jerk and tries to emulate the dexterity of his colleague. But when he tosses eggs into the air, they fall to the ground under his troubled gaze; the ice-cream sticks in the scoop, or if it does fly out, lands in the wrong glass. And when, with a professional flourish, he sends a glass scudding along the counter, it goes straight off the end and into the lap of a customer. A later scene in which he finds work as a coloured waiter involves the sort of colour jokes for which he never lost his innocent but unfortunate weakness.

Tossed in a blanket outside the bedroom window of the head of the women's college, Ronald's startled little face keeps appearing to the astonished lady's view, gazing at her curiously and as steadily as, in the circumstances, he may. When she attacks him,

College

in a womanly fashion, with her umbrella, he snatches it and, using it as a parachute, now floats in a more leisurely style as he comes and goes. Finally he makes a grab at the balcony, and he, she and it all come crashing down. At the fade, Ronald is just emerging from under the lady's vast skirts.

The track events, of course, were clearly Keaton's special delight. His efforts to emulate the college champions all end in disaster. Picking up the shot, he falls flat on his back. Sprinting, he is overtaken by two diminutive small boys. With the discus he succeeds in knocking off the dean's hat. The javelin falls four feet in front of him. The pole breaks as he attempts a vault; and after he has gone back and back and back into the far distance to get a good run-up for the high jump, the bar falls off before he even reaches it. He ends the long-jump with his head buried in the sand and his feet feebly kicking once or twice in the air; and floors himself with the hammer. The climax of this sequence is his

College

attempt at hurdling. With spectacular precision he knocks over every hurdle as he comes to it—except the last. Turning round at the finish he regards the ruin in astonishment; then, as much for the sake of neatness as out of pique, pushes over the last standing hurdle.

14: *Steamboat Bill Jr.*

For his last independently produced film Keaton returned to the theme which he had used in *The Saphead*, *The Navigator* and *Battling Butler* (and *College* too, to a degree): the effete youth who is extended by crisis and turns out in consequence and despite himself, a hero. The film was a total and unqualified success. The story is by Harbaugh again; and once more Keaton chose a setting of strong visual interest: an old-world Southern river town, reconstructed at Sacramento: 'The original story I had was about the Mississippi, but we actually used the Sacramento River in California, some six hundred miles north of Los Angeles. We went up there and built that street front, three blocks of it, and built the piers and so on. We found the river boats right there in Sacramento: one was brand new, and we were able to age the other one up to make it look as though it was ready to fall apart.'

The plot revolves around the rivalries of Steamboat Bill (Ernest Torrence) owner of the river-boat 'Stonewall Jackson,' and the rich banker, town boss and rival boat proprietor, King (Tom McGuire). Bill gets a telegram to say that his son, whom he has not seen since childhood, is coming back to visit him. Excited at the prospect of a partner, he goes to the railway station to meet his offspring. 'I bet he's bigger'n me now.' What he finds is an absurd little figure in huge bags and blazer, a ukulele under his arm, a terrible moustache and a ridiculous beret on top of his head. When Willie amuses a baby by skipping up and down and playing

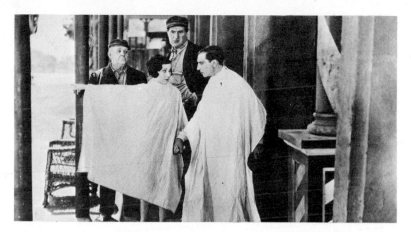

Steamboat Bill Jr., with Tom Lewis, Marion Byron, Ernest Torrence

his ukulele, Steamboat Bill threatens his mate: 'If you say what you're thinking, I'll strangle you.'

Steamboat Bill gets rid of his son's moustache and takes steps to improve his appearance, but worse is to come. His son is crazy about King's daughter, who was at college with him. The successive attempts of the youngsters to get together exacerbate the parents' enmities, while Willie's exceptional clumsiness causes considerable physical havoc both to the fathers and their boats.

King gets the 'Stonewall Jackson' condemned as unriverworthy; and when Bill assaults him, has him committed to gaol. Willie's attempts to slip a file to his father in a loaf of bread end disastrously. Avoiding arrest, Willie is knocked down by a car and taken to hospital. A great cyclone hits the town. The hospital is borne away and Willie and his bed are swept about the streets. After a series of escapes and adventures, a tree in which he is sheltering is seized by the wind and deposited in the river—just beside the deserted 'Stonewall Jackson.' The girl is swept by, on a floating house. Willie rescues her. Then the gaol-house floats by, the water up to Steamboat Bill's neck. Willie aims the 'Stonewall Jackson' head-on at the floating building and splits it asunder, rescuing his father from the water. Next he must dive in to rescue King, who is on the point of going down with his boat. All now seems to be well; but to the alarm of the girl and the astonishment of the two fathers, Willie dives in once more, to emerge a second later with—a parson.

Keaton—the most realistic and logical of comedians—has nevertheless a strong element of the surreal about him. But nowhere—not even in the overtly 'dreamed' films, *Convict 13*, *Playhouse* and *Sherlock Junior*—is there such a strong sense of nightmare as in the apocalyptic climax of *Steamboat Bill Jr*. Keaton's sudden and utter solitude is just as in a dream. After the first shots of people and cars being blown away no other soul is to be seen in the town as it suffers destruction. When Keaton leans forward at an angle of sixty degrees from the vertical to face the wind, and tries to walk, his efforts, like walking in a dream, only take him further away from his goal. The sense of dream is heightened, whether we recognise them or not, by references to Keaton's own memory. The town where he was born, Piqua, was blown right away by just such a cyclone; and people who knew him said that Keaton affected concern at having, in consequence, no birthplace. There was the childhood incident when he was himself carried by a whirlwind out of a window and deposited several streets away. There are other references to his vaudeville childhood: a sequence in an abandoned theatre where he encounters a magician's magic table and a ventriloquist's dummy. In the same theatre he mistakes a backdrop of a seascape for reality and attempts to dive into the water. Instead he slides down the drop, in just the way that he described his old vaudeville gag of the Original Aboriginal Dive. The dream continues to the end: nothing could be more dreamlike than the way the people of his life come floating along the river, on their personal ruins.

Oddly enough the cyclone was not Keaton's original idea for the climax of *Steamboat Bill Jr*.: 'My original situation in that film was a flood. But my so-called producer on that film was Joe Schenck, who at that time was producing Norma Talmadge, Constance Talmadge and myself, and who later became president

Steamboat Bill Jr.

of United Artists. Then later on 20th Century-Fox was Joe Schenck and his brother Nicholas Schenck was head man of M-G-M. Schenck was supposed to be my producer but he never knew when or what I was shooting. He just turned me loose.

'Well, the publicity man on *Steamboat Bill* goes to Schenck and he says: "He can't do a flood sequence because we have floods every year and too many people are lost. It's too painful to get laughs with." So Schenck told me, "You can't do a flood." I said, "That's funny, since it seems to me that Chaplin during World War One made a picture called *Shoulder Arms*, which was the biggest money-maker he'd made at that time. You can't get a bigger disaster than that, and yet he made his biggest laughing picture out of it." He said, "Oh, that's different." I don't know why it was different. I asked if it was all right to make it a cyclone, and he agreed that was better. Now, he didn't know it, but there are four times more people killed in the United States by hurricanes and cyclones than by floods. But it was all right as long as he didn't find out, and so I went ahead with my technical men and did the cyclone.'

The cyclone begins with the hospital building being lifted into the air, leaving Willie exposed in his hospital bed. The bed is swept along the streets and through lines of surprised horses in a livery stable. Willie steps out of his bed, which is promptly whirled away. At this moment comes the climax of the scene—the perfection of the gag which Keaton had proposed eight years before in *Back Stage* and polished in *One Week*, in which the complete side of a building crashes down around him, a window opening fortuitously and neatly fitting around him as he stands rigid and unaware. 'First I had them build the framework of this building and make sure that the hinges were all firm and solid. It was a building with a very tall V-shaped roof, so that we could make this window up in the roof exceptionally high. An average second storey window would be about 12 feet, but we're up about 18 feet. Then you lay this framework down on the ground, and build the window round me. We built the window so that I had a clearance of two inches on each shoulder, and the top missed my head by two inches and the bottom my heels by two inches. We mark that ground out and drive big nails where my heels are going to be. Then you put that house back up in position while they finish building it. They put the front on, painted it, and made the jagged edge where it tore away from the main building; and then we went in and fixed the interiors so that you're looking at a house that the front has blown off. Then we put up our wind machines with the big Liberty motors. We had six of them and they are pretty powerful: they could lift a truck right off the road. Now we had to make sure that we were getting our foreground and background wind effect, but that no current ever hit the front of that building when it started to fall, because if the wind warps her she's not going to fall where we want her, and I'm standing right out in front. But it's a one-take scene and we got it that way. You don't do those things twice.'

Keaton's co-director, Charles F. (Chuck) Reisner, was born in 1887 and had worked in vaudeville and as a song-writer and boxer before becoming a writer at Keystone in 1910. From 1918 to 1925 he had been assistant to Chaplin (and he was, incidentally, the father of the terrible little boy, Dinky Dean, in *The Pilgrim*). His other films as director—*Man on the Box, Caught Short, Reducing, The Better 'Ole* and so on—do not suggest that his contribution to the outstanding visual style of *Steamboat Bill Jr.* was greater than that of Keaton's co-directors to other films. He must have been a useful collaborator, though, for there is no question that the visual and technical qualities of the film are outstanding. The camera moves with an unobtrusive freedom which for its period is remarkable. 'We were moving cameras on elevators, on cranes, on rollers, and in all directions long before *The Last Laugh* was made. And that's the one that caused all the talk—*The Last Laugh*.' In particular the shooting of the scenes of altercation between the crews of the two rival boats, moored end to end, and the whole management of the cyclone sequence deserve attention.

One small scene is especially remarkable for a *mise en scène* of a simplicity and directness that recall Henry King. Willie is on the road on his way to visit his father in gaol. The girl appears some

Steamboat Bill Jr.: 'Willie exposed' →

distance behind him—seen, with Wellesian deep-focus again, in the depth of the field of vision. Willie turns and sees her; and she —having been on the point of addressing him—shyly turns and goes away. The total expressiveness and effectiveness of this economical scene is memorable.

Silly Willie's character is altogether enchanting. Central to it is the scene in which Steamboat Bill takes him to the hatter to try to find him a hat less offensive than his repellent beret. Willie's affection for the hat, however, is as powerful as Friendless's for Brown Eyes. He secretes the cap in his pocket. The only hat in the shop which seems to attract him is a cap almost as dreadful as the beret. He tries it on, but his father flings it off and slams a cowboy hat on his head. Willie retrieves the cap again; again it is cast off in favour of a homburg; next time—having been retrieved again— by a straw. The shot cuts to a side view of Willie looking into a mirror as a series of hats is planked on his head—the straw, a gaucho hat, another straw, a trilby, an upturned straw, a panama, an indescribable hat that is much too big. The shot cuts to a close-up of Willie looking directly into camera as if into a mirror. He plays with the brim of the hat for a moment; then suddenly the familiar Keaton flat hat appears and, with a quick, furtive, guilty look he snatches it off and hides it. At last they settle on a panama, but out in the street the first gust of wind carries it away, leaving Willie happily to get out his old beret again.

Generally, however, apart from the cyclone and the admirable scene in which Willie tries to smuggle the file to his father in gaol —Steamboat Bill at first will not even see his son, who has to communicate with the obtuse old man through comically elaborate signs and hints—it is less a film of extended sequence gags than of odd throwaways of rich absurdity: the nutshells on Willie's cabin floor which his father must negotiate in stocking-feet; the lifebelt that sinks as definitively as the 'Damfino's' anchor floated; and the silliest of Keaton's acrobatic gags. Steamboat Bill drags Willie off by the hand. A rigging wire rising up at forty-five degrees catches him under the crotch so that as Bill pulls Willie is forced up the wire.

15: M-G-M Productions: *The Cameraman* and *Spite Marriage*

'In 1928,' wrote Keaton, 'I made the worst mistake of my career. Against my better judgement I let Joe Schenck talk me into giving up my own studio to make pictures at the booming Metro-Goldwyn-Mayer lot in Culver City.' 'I'm just turning you over to my brother Nick,' Schenck told him. 'He'll take care of anything you want.' Chaplin and Lloyd both advised Keaton against the move; and Keaton himself knew that he would be 'lost making pictures in such a big studio'; but he was trapped into the deal.

He found his own old staff stolen away from him. 'When I went over to M-G-M I was again assured that every effort would be made to let me continue working with my team whenever possible. It turned out to be possible very seldom. . . . Usually, when I needed the old gang, one of them would be busy on a Norma Shearer picture, another on a Lon Chaney picture, and so on.'

There was no room at all for improvisation, which had been basic to his creation. The first idea Keaton took to Thalberg was a divine comic invention. 'Pretty much of a switch on *Steamboat Bill Jr.*,' it was set in the 1860s. Buster was to be a city namby-pamby sent to escort Marie Dressler west from Fort Dodge in a covered wagon. Keaton and Thalberg seem to have liked each other (Thalberg tried to get Keaton back to M-G-M after Mayer had fired him): but the boy wonder's judgement of comedy seems to have been shaky. Failing to see the endless Keatonian possibilities, he told him that the story was 'a little frail'; and the idea went no further than did a later suggestion for a parody of *Grand Hotel*, with Laurel and Hardy, Jimmy Durante, Marie Dressler (in the Garbo role of an ageing ballerina), Polly Moran, and with Keaton taking off the Lionel Barrymore role, as a man dying of hiccups and dutifully living up the forty years of life left to him.

Instead the studios proposed *The Cameraman*, the idea being (according to Keaton) that the film might indirectly publicise W. R. Hearst's newsreel company, in exchange for which the film might expect a good press from the Hearst papers. (Hearst was also a stock-holder in M-G-M.) Thalberg assigned his brother-in-law, Lawrence Weingarten, as producer; and Keaton, who had never worked with a script before, found himself with twenty-two official staff writers and a lot of amateur gagmen. Many weeks of tedious disagreement landed him with an elaborate script which, with Thalberg's nervous backing, he abandoned. Thalberg also agreed to override the studio decision that the film should be shot on location in New York, after this proved impracticable since Keaton was continually recognised and mobbed. After making a few establishing shots, the unit returned to Hollywood. Following an initial contest of authority, Keaton established an amiable working relationship with the director, Edward M. Sedgwick. Thus then, though not without months of a kind of battling to which he had never been accustomed, he secured for himself the sort of conditions he needed for creation. Unless to a degree in the making of *Spite Marriage*, he was never to manage it again.

The Cameraman betrays nothing of the struggle and strain that went into its preparation. It is a lucid, beautifully formed dramatic comedy. Buster is a street tintype photographer. He gets caught up in the crowds welcoming Gertrude Ederle after her Channel swim and watching her receive the key to New York from Mayor Jimmy Walker. (Here, as in the later scene involving Lindbergh's drive through New York, Keaton made use of actual news film.) Falling in love with Sally, an employee of the Hearst News company, he hocks his tintype camera to buy a vintage Pathé movie camera. On Sally's advice he tries to catch some news events which he can submit as freelance work. He mistakes a doorman for a general,

gets launched with a ship; and when finally he submits his work to the Hearst officials, it is a disastrous jumble of every technical error possible to the camera.

Sally nevertheless promises a date for the next Sunday; but their trip to Coney Island ends in catastrophe. A visit to the swimming-pool results in terrible confusions and embarrassments; and when they leave in the pouring rain, Sally goes off with Stagg, the crack cameraman and Buster's rival for her affections. Sally is the most loyal of Keaton heroines, however. She tips him off about a China-town festival that is going to develop into a tong war. Despite having unwillingly joined forces with an organ-grinder's monkey, he films the war and brings his spools back to the newsreel offices. Disaster again; for it seems he had no film in his camera.

The following day he films a regatta. Sally is in Stagg's boat, which overturns. The cameraman leaves his camera to rescue her; but when he goes to get medical aid, Sally revives and goes off with the cowardly Stagg, who allows her to suppose him to be her rescuer. Defeated at last, the cameraman trades in his movie camera and goes back to tintypes.

Meanwhile, however, two reels of his film have turned up by mistake in the newsreel projection-room. There on the screen, mysteriously, is the tong war after all. From an explanatory flash-back (a curious device but here entirely justified by its use) we learn that the clever monkey had removed the used reel and substituted a new one while the cameraman was not looking . . . and, habituated to the organ handle, had continued cranking after the cameraman had gone into the water to save Sally. All is revealed: Sally's danger; Buster's bravery; Stagg's cowardice and hypocrisy. In the final scene, the adoring Sally and the blissful cameraman are walking along Broadway. She tells him how much everyone admires him. Every window in every skyscraper suddenly opens and showers down confetti and ticker tape. The cameraman graciously acknowledges the acclamation: he is far too elated to suppose that the welcome is not in fact for him but for a fellow called Lindbergh in a car just behind.

Appropriately, *The Cameraman* seems to sum up all Keaton's

career. There are memories of earlier films. The Coney Island sequence (actually shot in Venice, California) recalls his fourth Arbuckle short. The ship launching echoes *The Boat*; the Police Parade and the hero's cheerful acceptance of the crowd's applause, *Cops*. He explores his complete range as a performer. The swimming-pool sequence is the apogee of low comedy. (The four-minute scene in the changing-room, in which Keaton and a cross fat man become horribly entangled in each other's clothing, was shot without rehearsal. The other player was Edward Brophy, the unit manager, who had never before acted but who as a result of this appearance subsequently made a career as a character actor.) Keaton's capacity for total expressiveness is nowhere better seen than in the Sunday morning sequence in which he is waiting for Sally to call and confirm their date. He is first glimpsed, all neat and ready in his Sunday best, sitting waiting by his bed. In an extraordinarily elaborate set-up, a precisely operated camera lift scans the cross-section of the five-storey house. When the bell rings, the hero hurtles downstairs, only to find the call is not for him. He climbs slowly back, up four flights of stairs, on to the roof, up the roof . . . The phone rings again; this time it *is* for him. He hurls himself down the stairs—four flights and into the coal-cellar. When he finally gets to the telephone and the girl tells him she is free, there could hardly be a more climactic celebration of joy. Leaving the telephone hanging, he bullets out of the house, through the New York traffic, up the steps and through the front door to stand there as she is putting down the receiver, bewildered that he did not say good-bye. 'Am I late?' he asks, shyly.

Like *Sherlock Junior*, *The Cameraman* is a film about film, though this time more about the making of films than the nature of the finished product. Keaton, the superb technician, fools with film and creates fun out of technical mistakes. His aside on the principles of *cinéma vérité* still seems valid. Caught in the Chinatown war, he is less concerned with saving himself than to secure good pictures. He bursts electric light bulbs to lure the battle within range of his lens; and when he finds two Chinese in a deadly

Spite Marriage

clinch, he slips a knife into one clutching hand to improve the scene. As a tyro cameraman, indeed, his resourcefulness is worthy of the shipwrecked Rollo Treadway.

People who have seen Keaton's last silent film, *Spite Marriage,* say that it shows no deterioration from the work of the great period that preceded it. Certainly its success at the time is indisputable. At the Empire Theatre in Leicester Square in May 1929, it broke all previous records—and this in competition with talking pictures. The subject, like *The Cameraman,* had been proposed by the studio, and Keaton again found himself fighting at every step with an army of writers and technicians, and above all with his producer —again Lawrence Weingarten. (It is interesting that Keaton himself wanted to use sound in this film; but the studio refused. Rudi Blesh offers the amusing idea that Irving Thalberg, conscious of Metro's investment in its single sound stage, boggled at Keaton's incautiously voiced theory that sound need not necessarily mean non-stop talking in pictures.) Again, however, it seems to have turned out an authentic Keaton film.

The hero is a trouser-presser in a tailor's shop, who develops a grand passion for a beautiful young actress. Borrowing finery from the shop, he haunts the stage door, until one night he lands a job as a super in the play in which his idol appears, a Civil War drama. Predictably his presence is enough to wreck the performance. To his surprise, however, the actress suddenly takes notice of him, and asks him to marry her. He is unaware that she is simply intent on spiting the *jeune premier* to whom she has been engaged. The bride drinks herself into a stupor, and the groom wrestles heroically through the night trying to get her to bed. The girl's former fiancé, her manager and her servants, all try to get rid of Buster. He foils their attempts to shanghai him, but somehow gets involved with a gang of bootleggers. Inexplicably but inevitably, he and his bride find themselves on a sinking yacht. Peril sparks off one of the old, heroic trajectories of action and impossible acrobatics; and at the end hero and heroine are happily reconciled in true love.

The sequence most frequently recalled is the bedroom scene in which Keaton devised something over a score of minute variations on the tricky problem of getting the girl's weighty and inert body on to the bed. Everyone who has seen the film remarks on the taste and discretion with which Keaton accomplished what could have been a rather dubious gag, though Weingarten, according to Keaton, tried to cut it: 'I don't want that type of thing in *my* pictures.' In later years other comedians borrowed the routine; and Keaton himself re-created it with his wife for the act they presented together at the Cirque Medrano. With singular aptness, an English trade review of *Spite Marriage* (in *The Bioscope*, 1 May 1929) summed up one of the central qualities in Keaton's whole comedy: "This is skilled in every detail *and helps to make impossibilities seem like reality.*'*

---

* Previous chapters in this book are based on recent viewings of the films. I have not seen *The Cameraman*, however, for nine years. *Spite Marriage*, obviously, I have never seen.

16: Exile from Creation

At thirty-three, Keaton's creative career was virtually at an end. At M-G-M he had lost the freedom which was the essential condition for his creation. At the same time unhappiness in his personal life had reached a critical stage. The change to talking pictures need not have been serious for him: he loved technical problems and could always find a solution to them. But he committed the almost suicidal error of offending Louis B. Mayer; and Mayer, who personally made a million dollars a year out of artists, seemed to delight in his power over them.

Keaton played in, but did not direct, a handful of sound features. Thereafter, most of the next quarter of a century was a terrible story of drink and sickness and failure: a disastrous marriage, work where he could get it in cheap shorts and tiny roles. Above all there was the uniquely refined torture—for a man of his compulsive creativity—of being deprived of the means of his art.

In his last years, life became kinder. He formed a happy marriage that lasted till his death. The money he was paid for the otherwise best-forgotten *Buster Keaton Story* restored his personal finances, and he found himself getting paid more for television appearances and commercials than he had received for the great features. In 1956 he ceased to drink. Recognition that had been so long delayed began to come with his successes at the Cirque Medrano, and culminated in the greatest ovation any artist has

On the set of *The Buster Keaton Story* (1956)

In the Good Old Summer Time (1949) and *The Railrodder* (1965)

ever received at the Venice Film Festival, when he appeared there in September 1965. By that time he had more offers of work than he could ever fulfil; and he seemed happy. He had the satisfaction of reclaiming and restoring, with the help of Raymond Rohauer, the prints of his old films.

By the time he came to play in Dick Lester's *A Funny Thing Happened on the Way to the Forum,* he was clearly very ill. For three months he was unable to work; though he did not know that he was suffering from a fatal cancer. Late on the afternoon of 31 January 1966 he was playing poker at his home when he suffered a seizure. His mind wandered, and he knew no one; but his body remained active and he would not lie down.* Early in the morning of 1 February he died.

---

* Information supplied by Raymond Rohauer.

17: Method and Mystery

From everything he said or wrote about his work we know that
Keaton's conscious aesthetic was reducible to two simple prin
ciples, in the pursuit of which he was as relentless and dogged and
single-minded as one of his own heroes: get a laugh; and don't be
too ridiculous.

Getting laughs, as we have seen, was a habit inbred in him. He
never knew any other *métier* or way of life. Gift and instinct were
combined here with a very conscious and exact judgement. He had
a clear idea of the ideal structure for his films: 'The best format I
found was to start out with a normal situation, maybe injecting a
little trouble but not enough to prevent us getting laughs. That
permitted us to introduce the characters getting in and out of
situations that were not too difficult. It was when we approached
the final third of the picture that we had the characters in serious
trouble which permitted bigger laughs, the biggest of all coming
when catastrophe threatens. I never repeated a gag or used the
same plot twice unless these could be so heavily camouflaged as to
be unrecognisable. Often the plot was based on a melodramatic
situation as in *The Navigator*. . . . But the situation need not be a
serious one. A good example of a light-hearted plot is *College*.'

With most comedians you can reduce gag structures to identifiable formulas and clichés. Keaton and Chaplin have in common
that everything they do seems new and spontaneous: their comedy
seems to be snatched from life as it passes, the response of an

original vision. Inevitably though there are certain orientations. Keaton finds inspiration in particular properties. Only a small minority of the films do not have trains or water (it was a maxim on the Keaton lot that a film would be a success so long as the boss was dunked). Cars, oddly enough, seem to have less appeal for him, though there is the dramatically collapsing Ford in *The Three Ages*, the courageous little Model Ts in *One Week* and *The Boat*; the amphibian convertible in *Sherlock Junior*; and several taxi-cabs worth recall. He enjoys jokes with dummies, with staircases, with centre-pivoted doors and with any kind of machine. He also (and though this is less attractive it is also so innocent as to be practically without offence) likes gags about Negroes and sometimes Jews.

Keaton has a very special fondness for animals and children, as if he finds in their innocence and singleness of purpose something nearer his own nature than adult human beings. In many films equine or canine drolls wander in for a scene or two; and of course the adorable Brown Eyes is Keaton's most dangerous co-star. Children are usually small Busters. The little boys in *The Boat* wear hats just like their father's and seem (in the mutual decision to hide the leathery pancakes for instance) to act in telepathic accord with him. In *The General* the train-driver's heels are dogged by two small fans who even follow him into Annabelle Lee's parlour when he goes to court her. But—being little Keatons—they are automatically set in motion when he reaches for his hat, and all he has to do is shut the door quickly before they realise he has sent them trotting out of it.

One or two gag types are recurrent. There is his favourite surprise effect of showing us an image which seems to have a certain meaning, and then giving us a larger view of the situation to reveal that we have been misled. The effect provides the opening for at least half a dozen of his films—*Cops, The Boat, The Balloon-atic, Sherlock Junior, Back Stage* (in Arbuckle days), and *My Wife's Relations* which begins with Buster apparently a sculptor, kneading clay. When the camera draws back we see that he is actually a confectioner, making humbugs. A variation of this is the delight in half-obscured messages. The hero of *Seven Chances* goes back-stage to propose to the beautiful actress on a poster outside the theatre. Only when he has gone in is a property basket removed to reveal the name of the performer—Julian Eltinge, the famous female impersonator. The plot of *The Navigator* springs on a similar accident; *Back Stage* has a particularly endearing joke on the same lines.

Keaton's pleasure in comic disproportion can first be observed in *The Cook*, where Arbuckle tries to put out a fire with teacups of water. Keaton often got laughs out of comparable disproportion of effort to intention. In any case he loved little things: the absurd little pistol in *Go West* or the tiny cannon which turns quite nasty and pursues him round the deck in *The Navigator*. In general Keaton has a special relationship with inanimate things. It has often been pointed out that the nature of his universe is that he is bedevilled by malevolent objects; but he could also tame them. No more intractable set of inanimate things could be found than the galley equipment in *The Navigator*; but how satisfactorily they are finally brought to heel. Keaton's kinship with objects comes less from the sympathy of an inanimate, mechanical man than from his ability to invest the things about him with distinct life and personality—not just the animals, but the little pistol, too, and the awful, but somehow irreproachably loyal beret in *Steamboat Bill Jr*.

Everyone who has seen the films remembers Keaton's gadgets. Making them seemed to be compulsive with him. His biographers recall the inventions he fixed up as a boy for the entertainment of fellow vaudevillians who rested at Lake Muskegon—one was a collapsible privy, another an elaborate waking-up machine like something from *The Scarecrow*. In the 1940s he created mad machines to amuse himself and two other outcasts from the M-G-M lot—Lucille Ball and Edward Sedgwick. Rudi Blesh quotes Lewis Jacobs' descriptions of huge and complex engines which went through operations as elaborate and solemn as the Emmett clock to reach a conclusion as elementary as raising a blind, cracking a nut or lighting a cigarette (this last machine carried its own box of matches, in case of failure). In his last home Keaton had made 'a miniature railroad that carries peanuts, soda pop, sandwiches, popcorn to guests seated around a small garden house near the pool.' (A pool naturally.) There is a special kind of mind (William Heath Robinson had such a one) which seems driven to create these abstractions of ingenuity, devices which use the logic of mechanics to deny logic. With Keaton it was also the same mind which absorbed the techniques of film-making until the craft was second nature, which created the inspired gadgetry of *The Electric House*, *The Scarecrow* or *The Navigator*, which perceived the senseless logic of all Buster's purposes, which conceived the greatest gags, that are enchainements of geometric and dynamic design. The climaxes of *Our Hospitality* and *Sherlock Junior* are not only jokes, but marvellous feats of engineering.

As a film-maker, Keaton worked with complete authority and autonomy. He expressed surprise at 'The lackadaisical working habits of many modern comedy stars. . . . We stayed with the story all of the way. In the old days all of us—Chaplin, Lloyd, Harry Langdon and myself—worked with our writers from the day they started on a story. We checked on the scenery, the cast, the locations. . . . We directed our own pictures, making up our own gags as we went along, saw the rushes, supervised the cutting, went to the sneak previews.' At no other time in the history of the cinema could an artist have enjoyed conditions of such creative freedom as the eight brilliant years in which Keaton made these nineteen shorts and twelve features—among which even the few failures would have been notable if another artist had made them. 'Well . . . I was an independent unit working in my own studio. My cameraman, my technical man, the entire staff—they're all under salary fifty-two weeks a year because I went for years—when I got into making feature-length pictures—only making two a year. One for spring release and one for fall release. Well it actually didn't make any difference to me when I put the camera up. We owned our own camera. We weren't renting it. We had all our own equipment, and so it was the thing, even after the picture

'A problem to be solved': *Our Hospitality*

was finished. I'm in the projection room looking at cut sequences put together, and maybe the cutter says, "That one is mistimed. Let's do that one over. Get those people back tomorrow." So that costs nothing. Well today, if you did that in a motion picture, you'd wreck the company!'

In retrospect such conditions seem Utopian. Keaton used his freedom discreetly. His comedies cost rather more than an average dramatic production; but even when there were elaborate scenes like the underwater sequence in *The Navigator*, or unforeseen expenses like a forest fire while shooting *The General*, he kept his budgets down to a steady $200,000 or $220,000 a feature. Since they never grossed less than a million, the cost seemed modest. Keaton worked quietly and methodically. He shot his two-reelers in three weeks. The features were shot in eight weeks and cut in two or three weeks. He never used a written script, apparently keeping an entire conception of the finished film in his head. He avoided rehearsal, which he felt impaired the freshness of performance, and made very few takes.

Naturally and instinctively, without any basis of theory, Keaton arrived at a wonderfully precise and lucid film style. It seemed to develop naturally out of his training, from infancy, to solve every specific problem of stagecraft, added to inborn technical ingenuity, a rare visual sense and a natural intelligence and lucidity which are reflected in all his recorded conversations. For him the problem of filming was simply to provide the most effective and explicit staging for his gags. The marvels of *mise en scène*—the staging of the river scene in *Our Hospitality* or the remarkable three-dimensional compositions in *Battling Butler* and *Steamboat Bill Jr.*—are without any more pretension than to be the most practical and effective narrative method.

His editing, too, is impeccable—the perfect timing of the trained vaudevillian. The great motor-cycle trajectory in *Sherlock Junior*, ending with the smack-smack-smack of the final dive through the gangsters' hut—is the work of a very great cutter. His desire to stage and show his feats just as they happened without any deceit led him to favour rather long takes (the water-feed sequence in

Sherlock Junior, for instance, lasts forty seconds and is done in a single shot). This, at a time when the influence of Griffith's rapid cutting was predominant makes his cutting distinctive; and Penelope Houston has pointed out that he thus 'hit on the technique which happens to be most in line with modern, or at least 1960s aesthetics.'

To this extent the form of Keaton's art was conditioned by the first principle: the need to get a laugh. The constant awareness that you must not be 'too ridiculous' (essentially because that way you will lose your laughs) at once extended and disciplined his work. It extended him to the degree that he was never content with the canvas sets and Hollywood back-lots that satisfied other comedians. His settings had to be real—the historical locations of *The General*, the marvellously evocative river town created for *Steamboat Bill Jr.*; even, far back, the authentic tenement alley of *Neighbors*. Props ('The Navigator,' 'The General,' 'The Rocket,' 'The Damfino') had to be authentic. Action and characters had to be believable and logical. In his autobiography he is slightly apologetic about the crazy gag with which he ends *Hard Luck*, and explains that he would never use such a fantastic piece of business in a feature, where everything had to be much more logical. But, once satisfied that a gag—the rocks in *Seven Chances* for instance —was possible, he would go to enormous lengths to stage it, though it meant breaking his neck (*Sherlock Junior*) or his ankle (*The Electric House*) or risking drowning (in practically every film).

His great gag enchainements are often extraordinary—the rescue in *College*, the climaxes of the modern story in *The Three Ages*, of *Our Hospitality*, of *Sherlock Junior* and *Steamboat Bill Jr.* —but they are not unrealistic or impossible, not 'too ridiculous,' *because Keaton does them*. This is the crux of the paradox of Keaton's work. A practical man, driven by this horror of the ridiculous, he is the great realist among the comedians. Yet he is a surrealist, too (perhaps surrealism has to exist beside realism). His imagination envisaged surreal happenings, and his phenomenal skills enabled him to realise his visions. Being, consciously,

Aspects of love: *Neighbors* and *Seven Chances*

a realist, he justifies his visions by framing them in dreams. It is dreams in *Convict 13* and *Sherlock Junior* which liberate the images of fantasy: the little convict bouncing up and down on the hangman's elastic rope; the cinema projectionist who emerges from sleep into a dream, then enters that other dream which is the cinema screen.

Buster Keaton, finally, was a very great actor, whose means were purified and stripped down to a perfect restraint, and a perfection of expression. When Gordon Craig described the perfect actor, the *über-marionette*, guided by 'the wires which stretch from divinity to the soul of the poet,' he was describing Keaton: 'When anyone draws a puppet on paper, he draws a stiff and comic-looking thing. Such a one . . . mistakes gravity of face and calmness of body for blank stupidity and angular deformity.'

Gravity and calm. The myth of the Great Stone Face is foolishness. James Agee, who did much to promote the myth, nevertheless saw how expressive Keaton's quiet could be, so that 'even a smile was as deafening as a yell.' He is the only silent comedian with whom you are never for a moment in doubt as to what his thoughts are. Recognising a problem to be solved, he will slightly

lower his brows, draw his chin back and slightly to one side like a
bull about to charge. When he finds himself beside his girl, and
she lays her head by accident on his shoulder, and he must
overcome the problem of where to put his arms, his passion is
tremendous: yet all betrayed in one prolonged, steady drooping of
the great calm eyelids.

What if he does not smile? Neither did Garbo. He told an inter-
viewer that he did not smile because he was concentrating on
what he was doing, that it was unconscious, and that he was
unaware of the omission until he saw the films for himself. In any
case, 'I had other ways of showing I was happy.' It is hard to
imagine a more climactic celebration of joy than the mad run to
reach the girl's side while she is still holding the phone on which
she has asked him round (*The Cameraman*). He acts with his whole
being. In mute long-shot he can be more acutely expressive than
most actors in talking close-up. In some of his funniest moments
he is no more than a twirling spot in the distance. *The Cameraman*,
again, has a marvellously pathetic moment when Keaton sinks to
his knees on the lake shore, finding that the girl he had rescued
from drowning has gone off with the other fellow—all seen in
long-shot.

The other great comedians tended to play one role only, the point of their films being to see what happened when their fixed and familiar character was placed in a particular situation or a particular setting. Keaton played many roles. The priggish Ronald in *College* is as different from the timid projectionist in *Sherlock Junior* as the self-assured hero of *Our Hospitality* from the melancholy Friendless. Bertie Van Alstyne, Rollo Treadway and Alfred Butler are all spoilt millionaires, but otherwise completely distinct characters. Keaton, with his sense of realism, had a very firm grasp on character; and one of his complaints against M-G-M and the multiplicity of writers there was that 'they warp your judgement in the role you're working.'

There are many Keatons; and yet eventually only one Buster. When these tried young men are eventually placed in exceptional circumstances and faced with exceptional problems—a rebel army, a drifting liner, a family feud, a girl to be won—they change and grow. And extended thus by adversity, rising to cope with practical difficulties, employing their resources of wit and ingenuity and intelligence and physical ability in order to equal fate and overtake it, they all blend into one, and become Buster. Buster, stumping along, stiff-legged, single-minded on some curious purpose and happily oblivious, in his abstraction, of the fate that is overhanging him in the form of a big cop or an impending landslide; or sauntering away from some suspected or known peril with affected nonchalance: then, with a quick inquiring turn of the head, breaking into a trot, a run, a bullet-like flight with his body all piston-rods and his head thrown back to streamline the flying machine he has become; or faced, as it seems with imminent death (*The Boat*, *The Navigator*), drawing down the heavy lids to shut out the view of those marvellous, haunting, haunted eyes . . . only to open them again with a flick of astonishment as he realises that fate has still another turn and maybe one that is less unkind; or glimpsed alone in an endless landscape; or realising, slowly and with puzzlement, that his hat is stuck on his head or his foot is caught in a hole or some other catastrophe has come upon him and will certainly get worse before it gets better; or seen as the still, calm and slightly bewildered centre of some frenzy of chaos of which he is the innocent and only cause. Or simply looking at you with those incredible, beautiful, agonising eyes that were like no one else's. The figure is unique and instantly recognisable. A quarter of a mile off, or enclosed in a diving-suit, he has only to stand there to be known. He is unique, and yet he is all of us. Just a man—very small in comparison with the universe which he inhabits yet certain of his ability to conquer his environment, to govern it eventually. Optimistic because he knows he will finally triumph and win the girl. Optimistic, because even if a dam breaks and a Niagara bursts over his head, he has his umbrella. Melancholy, because life is like that.

Such was Keaton's vision of Buster. Quite outside his own volition, and without relation, except by accident, to the circumstances of his own life, Keaton was impelled to realise this vision, and given the gifts to do so. For he was, ultimately, a poet and— whatever that may be—a genius. 'I have come from afar,' said Duse, 'and have faith in my star. That is all. I can say no more. Nor do I wish to know more.' 'I never realised,' wrote Keaton, 'that I was doing anything but trying to make people laugh when I threw my custard pies and took my pratfalls.'

Filmography of Silent Films

Abbreviations: *p.c.* production company; *p* producer; *d* director; *sc* script; *ph* photography; *l.p.* leading players.

1: Films Starring Roscoe (Fatty) Arbuckle

The Butcher Boy (1917)

Released through Paramount Famous Players-Lasky. *p.c.:* Comicque Film Corporation. *p:* Joseph M. Schenck. *d/sc:* Roscoe Arbuckle. *ph:* Elgin Lessley(?). *l.p.:* Arbuckle, Keaton, Al St John, Josephine Stevens, Arthur Earle, Agnes Neilson. 2 reels. Released 12.4.1917. Shot in New York.

A Reckless Romeo (1917)

This title is included in some filmographies (and J.-P. Lebel identifies its leading players as Corrine [*sic*] Parquet and Alice Lake along with Keaton, Arbuckle and St John), but there seems some doubt as to its ever having existed.

Rough House (1917)

Released through Paramount Famous Players-Lasky. *p.c.:* Comicque Film Corporation. *p:* Joseph M. Schenck. *d/sc:* Roscoe Arbuckle. *ph:* Elgin Lessley (?). *l.p.:* Arbuckle, Keaton, St John. 2 reels. Released 20.6.1917. Shot in New York.

His Wedding Night (1917)

Released through Paramount Famous Players-Lasky. *p.c.:* Comicque Film Corporation. *p:* Joseph M. Schenck. *d/sc:* Roscoe Arbuckle. *ph:* Elgin Lessley (?). *l.p.:* Arbuckle, Keaton, St John, Alice Lake, Josephine Stevens. 2 reels. Released 20.8.1917. Shot in New York.

Oh, Doctor (1917)

Released through Paramount Famous Players-Lasky. *p.c.:* Comicque Film Corporation. *p:* Joseph M. Schenck. *d/sc:* Roscoe Arbuckle. *ph:* Elgin Lessley (?). *l.p.:* Arbuckle, Keaton, St John, Alice Lake. 2 reels. Released 19.9.1917. Shot in New York.

Coney Island (1917)

Released through Paramount Famous Players-Lasky. *p.c.:* Comicque Film Corporation. *p:* Joseph M. Schenck. *d/sc:* Roscoe Arbuckle. *ph:* Elgin Lessley (?). *l.p.:* Arbuckle, Keaton, St John, Alice Lake, Stanley Pembroke. 2 reels. Released 11.10.1917. Shot in New York (Coney Island).

Out West (1918)

Released through Paramount Famous Players-Lasky. *p.c.:* Comicque Film Corporation. Paramount-Arbuckle. Presented by Joseph M. Schenck. *p:* Joseph M. Schenck. *d/sc:* Roscoe Arbuckle. *ph:* Elgin Lessley (?). *l.p.:* Arbuckle, Keaton, St John, Alice Lake. (Also, according to Lebel, Joe Keaton.) 2 reels.

Released 20.2.1918. Shot in California. Unless otherwise stated all subsequent films mentioned in this filmography were shot in or around Hollywood.

The Bell Boy (1918)

Released through Paramount Famous Players-Lasky. *p.c.:* Comicque Film Corporation. Paramount-Arbuckle. Presented by Joseph M. Schenck. *p:* Joseph M. Schenck. *d/sc:* Roscoe Arbuckle. *ph:* Elgin Lessley (?). *l.p.:* Arbuckle, Keaton, St John, Alice Lake, Joe Keaton, Charles Dudley. 2 reels. Released 7.3.1918.

Moonshine (1918)

Released through Paramount Famous Players-Lasky. *p.c.:* Comicque Film Corporation. Paramount-Arbuckle. Presented by Joseph M. Schenck. *p:* Joseph M. Schenck. *d/sc:* Roscoe Arbuckle. *ph:* Elgin Lessley(?). *l.p.:* Arbuckle, Keaton, St John. 2 reels. Released 6.5.1918.

Goodnight Nurse (1918)

Released through Paramount Famous Players-Lasky. *p.c.:* Comicque Film Corporation. Paramount-Arbuckle. Presented by Joseph M. Schenck. *p:* Joseph M. Schenck. *d/sc:* Roscoe Arbuckle. *ph:* Elgin Lessley (?). *l.p* · Arbuckle, Keaton, St John, Alice Lake, Joe Bordeau. 2 reels. Released 22.6.1918.

The Cook (1918)

Released through Paramount Famous Players-Lasky. *p.c.:* Comicque Film Corporation. Paramount-Arbuckle. Presented by Joseph M. Schenck. *p:* Joseph M. Schenck. *d/sc:* Roscoe Arbuckle. *ph:* Elgin Lessley (?). *l.p.:* Arbuckle, Keaton, St John, Alice Lake. 2 reels. Released 20.8.1918.

A Desert Hero (1919)

Released through Paramount Famous Players-Lasky. *p.c.:* Comicque Film Corporation. Paramount-Arbuckle. Presented by Joseph M. Schenck. *p:* Joseph M. Schenck. *d/sc:* Roscoe Arbuckle. *ph:* Elgin Lessley (?). *l.p.:* Arbuckle, Keaton, St John, Alice Lake. 2 reels. Released 13.6.1919.

Back Stage (1919)

Released through Paramount Famous Players-Lasky. *p.c.:* Comicque Film Corporation. Paramount-Arbuckle. Presented by Joseph M. Schenck. *p:* Joseph M. Schenck. *d/sc:* Roscoe Arbuckle. *ph:* Elgin Lessley (?). *l.p.:* Arbuckle, Keaton, St John, Alice Lake. 2 reels. Released 20.8.1919.

The Hayseed (1919)

Released through Paramount Famous Players-Lasky. *p.c.:* Comicque Film Corporation. Paramount-Arbuckle. Presented by Joseph M. Schenck. *p:* Joseph M. Schenck. *d/sc:* Roscoe Arbuckle. *ph:* Elgin Lessley (?). *l.p.:* Arbuckle, Keaton, St John, Alice Lake, Teddy (the dog). 2 reels. Released 13.10.1919.

The Garage (1919)

Released through Paramount Famous Players-Lasky. *p.c.:* Comicque Film Corporation. Paramount-Arbuckle. Presented by Joseph M. Schenck. *p:*

Joseph M. Schenck. *d/sc:* Roscoe Arbuckle. *ph:* Elgin Lessley (?). *l.p.:* Arbuckle, Keaton, St John, Alice Lake, Teddy (the dog). 2 reels. Released 15.12.1919.

Some Keaton filmographies (among them Rudi Blesh's) also include *A Country Hero*, which has similar production credits to the foregoing series, but which was not released until 13 December 1920—practically a year after Keaton had left Comicque. It seems likely that the film has become confused with *The Hayseed*, which is not included in the Blesh filmography.

It is thought that Elgin Lessley was cameraman on most, if not all of the Arbuckle-Keaton films; but it has not been possible to establish his credits with certainty.

Jean Havez, who worked with Keaton as a gagman from 1920 until 1925 (*Seven Chances*) seems to have been employed in a similar capacity at Comicque. Clyde Bruckman appears to have joined Keaton at some point in 1920 or 1921.

2: Metro Production

The Saphead (1920)

Released through Metro. *p.c.:* Metro. *p:* John L. Golden, Winchell Smith, Marcus Loew. *supervisor:* Winchell Smith ('Written and produced under the personal supervision of Winchell Smith'). *d:* Herbert Blaché. *sc:* June Mathis. Based on the play 'The New Henrietta' by Winchell Smith and Victor Mapes. *ph:* Harold Wenstrom. *l.p.:* Buster Keaton (*Bertie Van Alstyne*), William H. Crane (*Nicholas Van Alstyne*), Irving Cummings (*Mark Turner*), Edward Jobson (*Rev. Murray Hilton*), Edward Alexander (*Watson Flint*), Jack Livingston (*Dr George Wainwright*), Edward Connelly (*Musgrave*), Jeffrey Williams (*Hutchins*), Odette Tyler (*Mrs Cornelia Opdyke*), Carol Holloway (*Rose Turner*), Beulah Booker (*Agnes Gates*), Katherine Albert (*Hattie*), Helen Holte (*Henrietta Reynolds*), Alfred Hollingsworth (*Hathaway*), Henry Clauss (*The Waiter*). 7 reels. Released 11.10.1920.

3: Keaton Productions—Shorts

The High Sign (1920; released 1921)

Released through Metro Pictures Corporation. *p:* Joseph M. Schenck. *d/sc:* Buster Keaton, Eddie Cline. *ph:* Elgin Lessley. *l.p.:* Buster Keaton, Al St John. 2 reels. Released 11.4.1921.

One Week (1920)

Released through Metro Pictures Corporation. *p:* Joseph M. Schenck. *d/sc:* Buster Keaton, Eddie Cline. *ph:* Elgin Lessley. *l.p.:* Buster Keaton, Sybil Sealey, Joe Roberts. 2 reels. Released 30.9.1920.

Convict 13 (1920)

Released through Metro Pictures Corporation. *p:* Joseph M. Schenck. *d/sc:* Buster

Keaton, Eddie Cline. *ph:* Elgin Lessley. *l.p.:* Buster Keaton, Sybil Sealey. 2 reels. Released 4.10.1920.

The Scarecrow (1920)

Released through Metro Pictures Corporation. *p:* Joseph M. Schenck. *d/sc:* Buster Keaton, Eddie Cline. *ph:* Elgin Lessley. *l.p.:* Buster Keaton, Sybil Sealey, Al St John, Joe Roberts. 2 reels. Released 12.11.1920.

Neighbors (1920)

Released through Metro Pictures Corporation. *p:* Joseph M. Schenck. *d/sc:* Buster Keaton, Eddie Cline. *ph:* Elgin Lessley. *l.p.:* Buster Keaton (*The Boy*), Virginia Fox (*The Girl*), Joe Keaton (*The Boy's Father*), Joe Roberts (*The Girl's Father*). 2 reels. Released 20.12.1920.

The Haunted House (1921)

Released through Metro Pictures Corporation. *p:* Joseph M. Schenck. *d/sc:* Buster Keaton, Eddie Cline. *l.p.:* Buster Keaton, Virginia Fox, Joe Roberts, Eddie Cline. 2 reels. Released 7.2.1921.

Hard Luck (1921)

Released through Metro Pictures Corporation. *p:* Joseph M. Schenck. *d/sc:* Buster Keaton, Eddie Cline. *ph:* Elgin Lessley. *l.p.:* Buster Keaton, Virginia Fox, Joe Roberts. 2 reels. Released 14.3.1921.

The Goat (1921)

Released through Metro Pictures Corporation. *p.c.:* Buster Keaton Productions Inc. *p:* Joseph M. Schenck. *d/sc:* Buster Keaton, Mal St Clair. *ph:* Elgin Lessley. *l.p.:* Buster Keaton, Virginia Fox, Joe Roberts, Mal St Clair. 2 reels. Released 17.5.1921.

The Electric House (1921)

First version, abandoned as a result of Keaton's accident during shooting.

The Playhouse (1921)

Released through First National. *p.c.:* Buster Keaton Productions Inc. *p:* Joseph M. Schenck. *d/sc:* Buster Keaton, Eddie Cline. *ph:* Elgin Lessley. *l.p.:* Buster Keaton, Virginia Fox, Joe Roberts. 2 reels. Released 6.10.1921.

The Boat (1921)

Released through First National. *p.c.:* Comique Film Company Inc. Presented by Joseph M. Schenck. *p:* Joseph M. Schenck. *d/sc:* Buster Keaton, Eddie Cline. *ph:* Elgin Lessley. *technical director:* Fred Gabourie. *l.p.:* Buster Keaton, Sybil Sealey. 2 reels. Released 10.11.1921.

The Paleface (1921)

Released through First National. *p.c.:* Comique Film Company Inc. Presented by Joseph M. Schenck. *p:* Joseph M. Schenck. *d/sc:* Buster Keaton, Eddie

Cline. *ph:* Elgin Lessley. *technical director:* Fred Gabourie. *l.p.* · Buster Keaton. 2 reels. Released 17.12.1921.

Cops (1922)

Released through First National. *p.c.:* Comique Film Company Inc. Presented by Joseph M. Schenck. *p:* Joseph M. Schenck. *d/sc:* Buster Keaton, Eddie Cline. *ph:* Elgin Lessley. *technical director:* Fred Gabourie. *l.p.:* Buster Keaton, Virginia Fox, Joe Roberts. 2 reels. Released 15.2.1922.

My Wife's Relations (1922)

Released through First National. *p.c.:* Comique Film Company Inc. Presented by Joseph M. Schenck. *p:* Joseph M. Schenck. *d/sc:* Buster Keaton, Eddie Cline. *ph:* Elgin Lessley. *technical director:* Fred Gabourie. *l.p.:* Buster Keaton, Kate Price, Monty Collins, Wheezer Doll. 2 reels. Released 12.6.1922.

The Blacksmith (1922)

Released through First National. *p.c.:* Comique Film Company Inc. Presented by Joseph M. Schenck. *p:* Joseph M. Schenck. *d/sc:* Buster Keaton, Mal St Clair. *ph:* Elgin Lessley. *technical director:* Fred Gabourie. *l.p.:* Buster Keaton, Joe Roberts, Virginia Fox. 2 reels. Released 21.7.1922.

The Frozen North (1922)

Released through First National. *p.c.:* Buster Keaton Productions Inc. *p:* Joseph M. Schenck. *d/sc:* Buster Keaton, Eddie Cline. *ph:* Elgin Lessley. *technical director:* Fred Gabourie. *l.p.:* Buster Keaton, Freeman Wood, Bonnie Hill. 2 reels. Released 3.8.1922.

Day Dreams (1922)

Released through First National. *p.c.:* Buster Keaton Productions Inc. *p:* Joseph M. Schenck. *d/sc:* Buster Keaton, Eddie Cline. *ph:* Elgin Lessley. *technical director:* Fred Gabourie. *l.p.:* Buster Keaton, Renée Adorée. 3 reels. Released 28.9.1922.

The Electric House (1922)

Released through Associated First National. *p.c.:* Buster Keaton Productions Inc. *p:* Joseph M. Schenck. *d/sc:* Buster Keaton, Eddie Cline. *ph:* Elgin Lessley. *technical director:* Fred Gabourie. *l.p.:* Buster Keaton, Virginia Fox, Joe Keaton, Joe Roberts, Myra Keaton. 2 reels. Released 19.10.1922.

The Balloonatic (1923)

Released through First National. *p.c.:* Buster Keaton Productions Inc. *p:* Joseph M. Schenck. *d/sc:* Buster Keaton, Eddie Cline. *ph:* Elgin Lessley. *technical director:* Fred Gabourie. *l.p.:* Buster Keaton, Phyllis Haver. 2 reels. Released 22.1.1923.

The title should not be confused with *Balloonatics*, a Century Comedy directed by J. G. Blystone in 1917.

The Love Nest (1923)

Released through First National. *p.c.:* Buster Keaton Productions Inc. *p:* Joseph M. Schenck. *d/sc:* Buster Keaton. *ph:* Elgin Lessley. *technical director:* Fred Gabourie. *l.p.:* Buster Keaton. 2 reels. Released 6.3.1923.

4: Keaton Productions—Features

The Three Ages (1923)

Released through Metro Pictures Corporation. *p.c.:* Buster Keaton/Joseph M. Schenck Productions. *p:* Joseph M. Schenck. *d:* Buster Keaton, Eddie Cline. *sc:* Clyde Bruckman, Jean Havez, Joseph Mitchell. *ph:* William McGann, Elgin Lessley. *technical director:* Fred Gabourie. *l.p.:* Buster Keaton (*The Young Man*), Wallace Beery (*The Rival*), Margaret Leahy (*The Girl*), Joe Roberts (*The Girl's Father*), Lilian Lawrence (*The Girl's Mother*), Horace Morgan (*The Emperor*), Oliver Hardy. 6 reels. Released 25.7.1923.

Our Hospitality (1923)

Released through Metro Pictures Corporation. *p.c.:* Buster Keaton/Joseph M. Schenck Productions. *p:* Joseph M. Schenck. *d:* Buster Keaton, Jack G. Blystone. *sc:* Clyde Bruckman, Jean Havez, Joseph Mitchell. *ph:* Elgin Lessley, Gordon Jennings. *technical direction:* Fred Gabourie. *l.p.:* Buster Keaton (*Willie McKay*), Joe Roberts (*Joseph Canfield*), Natalie Talmadge (*His Daughter*), Joe Keaton (*Engineer*), Joseph Keaton Talmadge (*Willie as a Baby*), Kitty Bradbury (*Aunt Mary*). Leonard Chapman (*James Canfield*), Craig Ward (*Lee Canfield*), Ralph Bushman (*Clayton Canfield*), Edward Coxon (*John McKay*), Jean Dumas (*Mrs McKay*), Monty Collins (*Rev. Benjamin Dorsey*), James Duffy (*Train Guard*). 7 reels. Released 20.11.1923.

Sherlock Junior (1924)

Released through Metro Pictures Corporation. *p.c.:* Buster Keaton/Joseph M. Schenck Productions. *p:* Joseph M. Schenck. *d:* Buster Keaton, *sc:* Clyde Bruckman, Jean Havez, Joseph Mitchell. *ph:* Elgin Lessley, Byron Houck. *technical director:* Fred Gabourie. *costumes:* Clare West. *l.p.:* Buster Keaton (*Sherlock Junior*), Kathryn McGuire (*The Girl*), Joe Keaton (*The Girl's Father*), Ward Crane (*The Rival*), Jane Connelly, Erwin Connelly, Ford West, George Davis, Horace Morgan, John Patrick, Ruth Holley. 5 reels. Released 24.4.1924.

The Navigator (1924)

Released through Metro-Goldwyn Pictures Corporation. *p.c.:* Buster Keaton Productions Inc. Presented by Joseph M. Schenck. *p:* Joseph M. Schenck. *d:* Buster Keaton, Donald Crisp. *sc:* Clyde Bruckman, Jean Havez, Joseph Mitchell. *ph:* Elgin Lessley, Byron Houck. *technical director:* Fred Gabourie. *electrical effects:* Denver Harmon. *l.p.:* Buster Keaton (*Rollo Treadway*), Kathryn McGuire (*The Girl*), Frederick Vroom (*The Girl's Father, Owner of 'The Navigator'*), Noble Johnson (*Cannibal Chief*), Clarence Burton, H. M. Clugston. 6 reels (originally tinted). Released 14.10.1924.

Seven Chances (1925)

Released through Metro-Goldwyn Pictures Corporation. *p.c.:* Buster Keaton Productions Inc. Presented by Joseph M. Schenck. *p:* Joseph M. Schenck. *d:* Buster Keaton. *sc:* Clyde Bruckman, Jean Havez, Joseph Mitchell. Based on the comedy by Roi Cooper Megrue, produced by David Belasco. *ph:* Elgin Lessley, Byron Houck. *technical director:* Fred Gabourie. *l.p.:* Buster Keaton (*Jimmie Shannon*), Ray Barnes (*Billy Meekin*), Snitz Edwards (*The Lawyer*), Ruth Dwyer (*Mary Jones*), Frankie Raymond, (*Mary's Mother*), Jules Cowles, Erwin Connelly, Jean Havez (*Man on the Landing*). 6 reels; prologue originally in colour. Released 22.4.1925.

Go West (1925)

Released through Metro-Goldwyn-Mayer Pictures Corporation. *p.c.:* Buster Keaton Productions Inc. *p:* Joseph M. Schenck. *d/sc:* Buster Keaton, assisted by Lex Neal. *scenario:* Raymond Cannon. *ph:* Elgin Lessley, Bert Haines. *technical director:* Fred Gabourie. *electrical effects:* Denver Harmon. *l.p.:* Buster Keaton (*Friendless*), Howard Truesdale (*Owner of the Diamond Bar Ranch*), Kathleen Myers (*His Daughter*), Ray Thompson (*Foreman*), Brown Eyes (*Herself*). 7 reels. Released 23.11.1925.

Battling Butler (1926)

Released through Metro-Goldwyn-Mayer Corporation. *p.c.:* Buster Keaton Productions Inc. *p:* Joseph M. Schenck. *d:* Buster Keaton. *sc:* Paul Gerard Smith, Albert Boasberg, Charles Smith, Lex Neal. Adapted from the stage play of the same name by Stanley Brightman and Austin Melford. Adapted by Ballard McDonald. *ph:* J. Devereux Jennings, Bert Haines. *technical director:* Fred Gabourie. *electrical effects:* Ed Levy. *l.p.:* Buster Keaton (*Alfred Butler*), Snitz Edwards (*His Valet*), Sally O'Neil (*The Mountain Girl*), Walter James (*Her Father*), Bud Fine (*Her Brother*), Francis McDonald (*Alfred Battling Butler*), Mary O'Brien (*His Wife*), Tom Wilson (*His Trainer*), Eddie Borden (*His Manager*). 7 reels. Released 30.8.1926.

The General (1926)

Released through United Artists Corporation. *p.c.:* Buster Keaton Productions Inc. *p:* Joseph M. Schenck. *d/sc:* Buster Keaton, Clyde Bruckman. *adaptation:* Al Boasberg, Charles Smith. *ph:* J. Devereux Jennings, Bert Haines. *technical director:* Fred Gabourie. *l.p.:* Buster Keaton (*Johnnie Gray*), Marian Mack (*Annabelle Lee*), Glen Cavender (*Capt. Anderson*), Jim Farley (*General Thatcher*), Frederick Vroom (*Southern General*), Charles Smith (*Annabelle's Father*), Frank Barnes (*Annabelle's Brother*), Joe Keaton (*Union General*), Mike Denlin (*Union General*), Tom Nawm (*Union General*). 8 reels. Released 22.12.1926.

College (1927)

Released through United Artists. *p.c.:* Buster Keaton Productions Inc. *p:* Joseph M. Schenck. *supervisor:* Harry Brand. *d:* James W. Horne. *sc:* Carl Harbaugh, Bryan Foy. *ph:* J. Devereux Jennings, Bert Haines. *editor:* J. S. Kell. *technical director:* Fred Gabourie. *l.p.:* Buster Keaton (*Ronald*), Ann Cornwall (*Mary Haines*), Harold Goodwin (*Jeff Brown*), Snitz Edwards (*Dean

Edwards), Florence Turner (*Ronald's Mother*), Flora Bramley (*Mary's Friend*), Buddy Mason (*Jeff's Friend*), Grant Withers (*Jeff's Friend*), Carl Harbaugh (*Boat Crew Trainer*), Sam Brawford (*Baseball Trainer*), Lee Barnes (*Keaton's Double for pole vault*). 6 reels. Released 10.9.1927.

Steamboat Bill Jr. (1928)

Released through United Artists. *p.c.:* Buster Keaton Productions Inc. *p:* Joseph M. Schenck. *d:* Charles F. (Chuck) Reisner. *sc:* Carl Harbaugh. *ph:* J. Devereux Jennings, Bert Haines. *editor:* J. Sherman Kell. *l.p.:* Buster Keaton (*Willie*), Ernest Torrence (*Steamboat Bill*), Tom Lewis (*His Mate*), Tom McGuire (*King*), Marion Byron (*King's Daughter*), Joe Keaton (*Barber*). 7 reels. Released 2.6.1928.

5: Metro-Goldwyn-Mayer Productions

The Cameraman (1928)

Released through M-G-M Distributing Corporation. *p.c.:* M-G-M. *p:* Buster Keaton. *d:* Edward Sedgwick. *sc:* Story by Clyde Bruckman, Lew Lipton; continuity, Richard Schayer. *ph:* Elgin Lessley, Reggie Lanning. *editor:* Hugh Wynn. *technical director:* Fred Gabourie (?). *l.p.:* Buster Keaton (*Buster*), Marceline Day (*Sally*), Harry Gribbon (*Cop*), Harold Goodwin (*Stagg*), Sidney Bracy (*Editor*). 8 reels. Released 15.9.1928.

Spite Marriage (1929)

Released through M-G-M Distributing Corporation. *p.c.:* M-G-M. *p:* Joseph M. Schenck. *d:* Edward Sedgwick. *sc:* story, Lew Lipton; adaptation, Ernest S. Pagano; continuity, Richard Schayer. *ph:* Reggie Lanning. *editor:* Frank Sullivan. *technical director:* Fred Gabourie (?). *l.p.:* Buster Keaton (*Elmer Edgemont*), Dorothy Sebastian (*Trilby Dew*), Edward Earle (*Lionel Benmore*), Leila Hyams (*Ethel Norcrosse*), Will Bechtel (*Frederick Nussbaum*), John Byron, Hank Mann. 9 reels. Released 22.4.1929.

French version: *Buster se Marie* (1929). *d:* Claude Autant-Lara. *l.p.:* Keaton, Mona Goya, Françoise Rosay.

Acknowledgements

I have quoted extensively from Keaton's own statements about his work. These, which are not always individually acknowledged in the text, come from Keaton's autobiography, *My Wonderful World of Slapstick* (published in Great Britain by Allen and Unwin, 1967); from Rudi Blesh's *Keaton* (published in Great Britain by Secker and Warburg, 1967); from interviews with Christopher Bishop (*Film Quarterly*, fall 1958), with Kevin Brownlow (*Film*, No. 42), with John Gillett and James Blue (*Sight and Sound*, winter 1965–66), with Arthur B. Friedman (*Film Quarterly*, summer 1966); and certain private and unpublished interview material.

The primary debt of anyone who loves Keaton is to Raymond Rohauer, who over the last fifteen years of Keaton's life helped him to trace and restore the pictures of his great silent period; and who has subsequently made them available, with the co-operation of Keaton's executor, Leopold J. Friedman. Miss Brenda Davies and her staff in the Information Department of the British Film Institute, and especially Gillian Hartnoll, the National Film Archive's book librarian, have been outstandingly generous with their help. Kevin Brownlow's advice is indispensable to anyone dealing with silent cinema. In particular, however, I am grateful to the projection staff of the National Film Theatre—Alf Francis, Tony Sweatman, Bob McCarthy, Alf Squires—whose patience is staggering and whose suggestions, if sometimes caustic, are always creative.

For stills, I am indebted to the National Film Archive, and to Kevin Brownlow and John Kobal.

DATE DUE